P9-CAE-738

About the author

Darren Main is a yoga and meditation instructor and author. His books *include Yoga and the Path of the Urban Mystic, Spiritual Journeys along the Yellow Brick Road,* and *The Findhorn Book of Meditation.* In addition to writing, he facilitates workshops and gives talks on yoga and modern spirituality throughout the United States and abroad and is the director of the Yoga Tree Teacher Training Program. He currently lives in San Francisco.

www.darrenmain.com

Hearts & Minds

Talking to Christians about Homosexuality

Darren Main

FINDHORN PRESS

© Darren Main 2008

The right of Darren Main to be identified as the author of this work has been asserted by him in accordance with the Copyright, Designs and Patents Act 1998.

First published by Findhorn Press 2008

ISBN 978-1-84409-145-4

A CIP catalogue record for this book is available from the British Library.

Edited by Judith Cope
Cover design by Jasper Trout
Layout by Thierry Bogliolo
Printed in the USA

1 2 3 4 5 6 7 8 9 10 11 12 13 14 13 12 11 10 09 08

Published by
Findhorn Press
305A The Park,
Findhorn, Forres
Scotland IV36 3TE

Tel +44(0)1309 690582
Fax +44(0)1309 690036
eMail: info@findhornpress.com
www.findhornpress.com

Contents

Pride viii

Introduction 1

Part One *Love Thy Neighbor, Love Thy Self* 7

Chapter 1 Spiritual Armor 8

Chapter 2 Daily Spiritual Practice 18

Chapter 3 Speaking Truth to Power 22

Part Two *The Truth Shall Set You Free* 31

Chapter 4 Fear Not the Bible 32

Chapter 5 Literalist vs. Figurative Bible Study 47

Chapter 6 Knocking King James off His Throne 57

Chapter 7 The Purity Laws 63

Chapter 8 The Sins of Sodom 71

Chapter 9 Saint Paul's View of Homosexuality 78

Chapter 10 Jesus and Homosexuality 84

Chapter 11 Love Stories 96

Conclusion 104

Part Three—Essays: Touched by Religious Intolerance 111

The Dream of a New Language *by Laura C. Engelken* 113

Just A Little Patience *by Jasper Trout* 116

God and Gays *by Luane Beck and Kim Clark* 122

Religious and Spiritual Healing *by James Guay* 127

Leaving the Church and Finding Love *by Kathy Ascare* 131

Reconciled *by Jason Warner* 133

Healing from the Broken Truth *by Darlene Kay Bogle* 140

Two Thousand Years Later *by Darren Main* 145

Resources 147

Appendix A Recommended Reading 148

Appendix B Recommended Films & Music 150

Appendix C Queer-friendly Organizations and Websites 151

Acknowledgments 155

green
press
INITIATIVE

Findhorn Press is committed to preserving ancient forests and natural resources. We elected to print this title on 30% post consumer recycled paper, processed chlorine free. As a result, for this printing, we have saved:

12 Trees (40' tall and 6-8" diameter)
4,428 Gallons of Wastewater
8 million BTU's of Total Energy
569 Pounds of Solid Waste
1,067 Pounds of Greenhouse Gases

Findhorn Press made this paper choice because our printer, Thomson-Shore, Inc., is a member of Green Press Initiative, a nonprofit program dedicated to supporting authors, publishers, and suppliers in their efforts to reduce their use of fiber obtained from endangered forests.

For more information, visit www.greenpressinitiative.org

Environmental impact estimates were made using the Environmental Defense Paper Calculator. For more information visit: www.papercalculator.org.

Dedicated to Michel Lynch, Richard Schwass and Robert Bankel for giving me permission to love myself and to Jasper Trout for teaching me how to love another man. Without each of you, I would not be the man I am today and this book would never have come into being.

Pride

There is an axiom that only a fool is proud of what he can't help being. I was lucky to have been born gay, but that evokes a sense of gratitude, not pride. For me, pride is the result of commitment, accomplishments and character.

I feel pride when I see queer people making the world more beautiful, or responding to prejudice against us with dignity and compassionate strength.

I feel pride when I see young queer people taking a same-sex date to the prom, or two lesbians getting married for the first time in Massachusetts.

I feel pride when we play sports together, do charitable works together, pray and meditate together, and sing together.

Most importantly I feel pride when we stand up and make our voices heard in Washington, DC and in state capitols all around this country.

We are no longer a bunch of queer individuals living in individual closets of hell. We are a community. Our community is filled with many problems and challenges, to be sure, but the fact that we stand together means that we no longer have to suffer alone.

To me, that is worth marching in the streets.

—Darren Main
San Francisco, California, June 2002

Introduction

I was a senior in high school when I first came out publicly. Prior to that, I had only come out to a few friends. I had always dated women, and even enjoyed sexual relationships with them, but I also had an eye for men. I had been struggling to stay clean and sober and was about one year into my sobriety when I embarked on a school trip to Europe.

On one of the last nights of the trip, a group of us were playing *truth or dare* in a hotel in Venice. All the usual embarrassing questions were being tossed around the room, and when it came to me, I was asked the inevitable question about gay sex. My first instinct was to lie; it was self-preservation, after all. But something inside of me snapped. I was tired of lying and feeling ashamed. I was tired of hiding. In my twelve-step work, I had been addressing the issue of honesty. So instead of doing what I had done so many times before, I opened my mouth and told the truth.

The room fell silent. I half expected to be dumped in one of the canals of Venice and left for dead. Instead, one by one, people began to smile. Some nodded their heads in a gesture of approval. A few of the girls even voiced their support. One person, though, was notably stoic.

His name was George, and he will be forever burned in my memory as the first Christian to try to save me from the "sin of homosexuality." To his credit, he waited until we were alone to tell me what a sinner I was. But that was where his thoughtfulness ended. In order to "save" me, he used every tactic he had to try to convince me

I was going to hell if I didn't repent and accept Jesus. I heard about "Adam and Steve" and about "Sodom and Gomorrah." I was told that homosexuality was "against nature" and that he "loved the sinner but hated the sin." He tossed out Bible verse after Bible verse to try to convince me that I was on the fast track to hell.

I had nothing to say in return. I was no Bible scholar, but I did know that God did in fact make Adam and Eve, not Adam and Steve. As to the many other Bible verses, I had not heard most of them, but they did seem fairly damning. Not having an answer to the case he was making, I did what any bitter and angry young man would do—I yelled back at him that "the Bible is all bullshit anyway!"

Needless to say, things went south from there. George yelled back and things turned into a heated argument. In the end, he didn't "save" me, and I didn't change his mind about homosexuality. We both parted a whole lot angrier and still feeling that the other was wrong.

George was the first in the long line of Christians with whom I would have this debate—a debate that might as well have been pre-recorded because it always went down the same way. The Christian du jour would start off with a soft and soothing voice and usually focused on Jesus' love. I would make a comment about Jesus' loving all people, including homosexuals. They would toss out the same Biblical verses and I would tell them that the Bible was bullshit. Then came the heated arguments in which each of us would only listen to ourselves. We would end in a huff, and nothing would change.

Hearts and Minds

It took me years to realize that these arguments were neither healthy nor helping anyone. It was only when I
started to get my own anger under control and began to
use facts and logic that I started to see the occasional
change of heart. The one thing that George had, as did
many of the Christians that followed him, was genuine
concern for me. True, he was just parroting back to me
the same old tired lines that were fed to him by someone
else. But in his eyes, there really was deep concern.
George was not a bad man. He was misguided, in my
opinion, but a genuinely good person. Had I not yelled
at him and had I discussed with him the Bible with calmness and logic instead of calling it bullshit, there is a
good chance his own thinking would have begun to
change on this issue.

I could not do any of that, however, because I didn't
know the Bible and I was angry going into the conversation. It took me many years to refine my skills and gain
the knowledge needed to have a thoughtful and meaningful discussion with Christians. This book is the cul-
mination of these efforts. It is intended to be both a
guide and a resource for people who want to help
Christians open their hearts and minds rather than slamming that door shut in anger.

Much has been made lately of the so-called "culture
wars" that are dividing our society. Issues such as abortion, gay marriage, stem cell research and school prayer
are at the heart of this war. As with any war, this is one
that cannot be won in ignorance and fear. We can only
succeed in winning the war by changing hearts and

minds. If the Iraq war has shown us nothing else, it is that "might doesn't always make right" and without the hearts and minds element, the war will wage on without end.

It is time for us to end this culture war with Christians by understanding their positions and helping to educate the many open-minded Christians to the fact that gays, lesbians and all queer and transgender people have a place at the table. Beyond the fact that we have the civil right to be at the table, it is what Jesus likely would have wanted, and thus acceptance of the queer community is a very Christian ideal.

This book is a guide to help you talk to your Christian friends and family in a way that both honors their faith and empowers them to open their hearts and minds. It is a book about ending this silly war between the queer and Christian communities. It is a book for queer men and women and the many people who love and support us and who want to take a stand against religious intolerance. It is a book that will hopefully invite many in the Christian community to revisit the practice of tolerance and compassion that is at the center of Christ's teachings, and help them learn to apply those principles to members of the queer community.

This book is divided into three parts. The first part will deal with the rift we find between the queer community and many Christian churches. Most churches that disapprove of homosexuality make no secret of this. But the intolerance is not just one sided. Many queer men and women as well as the straight friends and families who support us have a lot of intolerance toward Christians in general. My hope is to address this issue right up front. Learning to respect people with different views is one of the greatest tools we have in disarming hostility and inviting others to open their hearts and minds.

In Part Two, we will be looking carefully at the Bible. Obviously the Bible is used by many Christians to justify their disapproval of homosexuality. A handful of verses are often used to back up the belief that being queer is a sin. Before we can honestly understand these passages we need to understand the Bible as whole. One of the reasons some Christians believe that we are sinners is because they have taken Bible verses out of context. In this section we will look at each of these passages and try to figure out what they really say.

In Part Three, I will share essays from a variety of queer and queer-friendly people whose stories are both touching and inspiring. These essays are there to support you. I have found that knowing you are not alone can make all the difference. You are welcome to share these inspirational essays with others and to contact their authors.

I have written this book with a number of folks in mind. Obviously queer men and women will find the information useful when they encounter Christians who want to "save" them. It is always nice to enter such conversations armed with a bit of knowledge.

Additionally, friends and family members may want to "defend" their queer loved ones. It is only natural for parents, siblings and friends to want to defend their loved ones. It is my hope that this book will help them in doing just that.

Lastly, this book is for queer Christians. Many queer

individuals have felt they need to choose between their faith and their sexuality. For these people, the war between Christianity and homosexuality is not something being waged in arguments with others; it is an internal conflict. It is my deepest hope that this book will help you end that internal debate so that you can embrace and integrate all parts of who you are.

One last thought: this book is by its very nature controversial. Even people who agree with me that homosexuality and modern Christianity are not in conflict may disagree with my presentation of Scripture and my characterization of some Christians and their theology.

Obviously there is tremendous room for interpretation when it comes to any issues around spirituality, sacred texts, and theology. I have not written this book as the final word on the subject of homosexuality and Christianity. In fact, my hope is just the opposite—that this book will start a rich discussion that will facilitate healing and reconciliation.

—Darren Main
San Francisco, CA
www.darrenmain.com

Part One

Love Thy Neighbor, Love Thy Self

As human beings, our greatness lies not so much in being able to remake the world—that is the myth of the atomic age—as in being able to remake ourselves.

—MOHANDAS GANDHI

Chapter One

Spiritual Armor

The greatness of this period was that we armed ourselves with dignity and self-respect. The greatness of this period was that we straightened our backs up because a man can't ride your back unless it is bent.

—THE REV. MARTIN LUTHER KING, JR.

By the time I was twenty-five, I had come out to everyone in my family except for my father. My sexuality was not an obvious issue as I was still dating women. My mother, brother and sister all knew I had been involved with men, and had very little difficulty accepting that.

I saw no good reason to tell my father because I did not have a lot to report—I had not been in a serious romantic relationship with a man. My father, one of the most decent and honest men I know, is also very old-fashioned. While he does not practice a specific religion, his values are very traditional.

My father grew up on a farm with eight brothers, all of them very good men, but also very "small-town" in their views of homosexuality. Growing up, I remember my father talking about the Anita Bryant case, in which the famous country singer led protests against gays teaching school. Her career was ruined as a result of her protests

and the boycotts that ensued. My father much supported her position and was very vocal about this on a number of occasions.

He also worked with a man named Joe who was
thought to be gay. Behind Joe's back, and perhaps even
to his face, everyone called him "Josie." It was not that
my father would deliberately hurt anyone, but his views
and attitudes were such that I knew my coming out
would not go over well.

Eventually, I did fall in love with a man. It was a beautiful time in my life and I wanted to share it with my
family. I had no fears that most members of the family
would not accept my relationship with Jasper, but given
my father's closed mind about homosexuality, I had serious concerns that the news of my being queer would sig-
nificantly hurt our relationship.

I waited until I was home for a visit to spring the news.
Fortunately, this gave me a few months to meditate on
the issue and become more centered and grounded.
Thankfully, yoga and meditation had become an important part of my life. In hindsight, taking the time to get
comfortable with myself was one of the most important
things I had ever done in regard to my relationship with
him.

The day came. I picked up my dad so we could go to
the local coffee shop to catch up. I decided to tell him
while we were still in the car so as to afford the most privacy possible.

"Dad," I said, "I have some news. I am in a great relationship."

"That's wonderful!" he replied.

"It's with a man," I said with a confidence that surprised me.

"That's no good. I mean, that goes against nature." He continued on along these lines for a while.

After a few moments, I interrupted. "Dad, I'm not telling you this because I want your permission or even your approval. I know that is not likely. I'm telling you this because I am in love and I am happy. You are my father and I love you. I just thought it was important that you know."

He fell silent for a minute. "Well, you're right in that it is not likely that I'll ever understand or approve, but it's your life and I only want you to be happy."

Now, this conversation could have gone much worse. I could have gone into the situation seeking his approval. I could have demanded he understand. I could have called him old-fashioned and demanded that he open his mind. If I had done that, I have no doubt it would not have gone so well. I would not have changed his mind and I would likely have driven him further away.

This event in my life taught me something very, very important. When one goes into a situation with an attachment to the outcome, it is almost certain that things will turn to chaos, but when one enters a discussion without attachment to the outcome, he or she is free to draw on the logic and reason that only a calm and unattached mind can access.

A few months ago one of my students emailed me the following parable:[1]

---

[1] The author of this parable is unknown. It has circulated around the Internet in various forms for several years.

Years ago, a farmer owned land along the Atlantic seacoast. He constantly advertised for hired hands. Most people were reluctant to work on farms along the Atlantic. They dreaded the awful storms that raged across the Atlantic, wreaking havoc on the buildings and crops. As the farmer interviewed applicants for the job, he received a steady stream of refusals.

Finally, a short, thin man, well past middle age, approached the farmer. "Are you a good farm hand?" the farmer asked him. "Well, I can sleep when the wind blows," answered the little man.

Although puzzled by this answer, the farmer, desperate for help, hired him. The little man worked well around the farm, busy from dawn to dusk, and the farmer felt satisfied with the man's work. Then one night the wind howled loudly in from offshore. Jumping out of bed, the farmer grabbed a lantern and rushed next door to the hired hand's sleeping quarters. He shook the little man and yelled, "Get up! A storm is coming! Tie things down before they blow away!"

The little man rolled over in bed and said firmly, "No sir. I told you, I can sleep when the wind blows."

Enraged by the response, the farmer was tempted to fire him on the spot. Instead, he hurried outside to prepare for the storm. To his amazement, he discovered that all of the haystacks had been covered with tarpaulins. The cows were in the barn, the chickens were in the coops, and the doors were barred. The shutters were tightly secured. Everything was tied down.

Nothing could blow away. The farmer then understood what his hired hand meant, so he returned to his bed to also sleep while the wind blew.

In many ways, this parable reflects the situation we find ourselves in with regard to queer issues and Christianity. Many of us simply avoid the issue of homosexuality within religion because it so often makes us uncomfortable. As the world has become more gay-friendly, it has become much easier for us to surround ourselves with people who share many of our own beliefs and values about homosexuality. Yet even in this environment, you will occasionally find your beliefs about homosexuality under attack.

Maybe it will be your Christian parents, or your Evangelical co-worker. Maybe it is your brother or an in-law who makes an insensitive statement. Storms will come, and in a democratic society we must learn to contend with different points of view.

The question, of course, is not whether the storms will come, but rather how prepared we will be when they do. Once we are grounded in our beliefs, the winds of intolerance will howl, but we will no longer have to become ruffled. Rather than react to ignorant and unfounded statements, we can calmly state our case and plant the seeds of tolerance.

In order for us to stand tall and speak truth, we need to heal ourselves first. I have often felt that the biggest gay-bashers around are in the queer community itself. How many queer people are beaten up or killed every year in hate crimes? According to the FBI[2], in 2004 there were 1,197 reported incidents of violence based on sexual orientation. Yet when you compare that number to the copious amount of people in the queer community who are addicted to hard drugs such as crystal meth, or

---

[2] FBI, "Crime in the United States," 2004

on should have to. Robertson's inflammatory, false and misleading statements are enough to make one's blood boil. Yet to allow myself to become angry is to fall into his trap, because the more we yell and scream, the more our detractors will view us as insane.

There is no doubt that we must "[arm] ourselves with dignity and self-respect." Failure to do this will only lead to more anger and fear and we will never feel as though we have a place at the spiritual table. Just as Martin Luther King, Jr. helped lead the civil rights movement by inspiring people to feel good about themselves and to stand peacefully in truth, we must do the same.

Oppression is never overcome by outside forces. It is delusional to think that Pat Robertson is going to wake up one day and decide that homosexuals are loved by God and deserve equal treatment. Every stride we have made in the quest for queer rights has come only beyond the doorway of increased personal power. Be it Stonewall[4] or the San Francisco "White Night" riots,[5] every great leap we have made has only come when we stood tall and refused to take a metaphorical seat at the back of the bus!

It is my strong belief that our next step is to come fully to the spiritual table. Not because we are invited by the

---

The Stonewall riots took place at a gay bar in New York. On June 28, 1969 the police were once again conducting a sting operation in which they would arrest people for being queer. What made this night different was that people refused to take it. They stood up and fought back. Thus began the queer civil rights movement.

On November 27, 1978, San Francisco Board of Supervisors member Harvey Milk was gunned down for being gay by Dan White, a fellow city supervisor. White was given a very light sentence because of the now-famous "Twinkie Defense." This provoked outrage in the queer community, which resulted in riots. Over 150 people were injured that night, but it is largely seen as another big step in the quest for civil rights.

to the numbers of suicides among queer people,
clear that many queer individuals don't think too r
of themselves.

Granted, many of us do not have hardcore drug ¡
lems. But far too many do. On some level, we fee
than others and unworthy of happiness. Interna
homophobia can and will be exploited by the reli§
right. Take, for example, these very "Christian" w
spoken by Pat Robertson:

> "You know, one of the great misnomers in our
> society is the term "gay." That somebody who is
> involved in something that is leading to suicide,
> where the V.D. rate is 11 times that of others, which
> are almost driven and ashamed and fearful and
> confused and psychotic and all the others that we
> read about plaguing this part of our society. The
> term gay is the most serious misuse of the English
> language. They're not gay, they're very, very
> depressed and miserable."[3]

The sad part is that while he is misusing statistic:
as a community need to look at much of what he i§
ing—not because he is speaking the truth, but be(
our choices about how we live our lives ca¡
unhealthy and the results can be devastating to our
munity.

When the suicide rate is as high as it is and drug
and STDs are huge issues, we get hit with a d(
whammy. First we injure ourselves, and then rel:
extremists pick up the same stick and beat us w
again.

As I have researched this book, I have had to e
more sentiments like Pat Robertson's than any or

---

[3] Spoken on his national TV show The 700 Club, May 6, 1982

religious right, but because it is our God-given right to sit there. Unfortunately we have largely given up our voice in this area. We have let the religious right claim to be the moral authority for far too long, when there is nothing moral about denying queer people equal rights or sending young people to ex-gay "rehabilitation" centers. There is nothing moral about protesting gay funerals or not allowing queer couples to marry.

None of this will change until we stand up in significant numbers and confront the lies that are being trumpeted from so many Christian pulpits. In order to do this, we must, as Dr. King suggests, "[arm] ourselves with dignity and self-respect." In regard to Christian intolerance, our best means of doing this is through logic and reason—talking to one Christian at a time until it is no longer acceptable to gay bash from the pulpit.

How do we arm ourselves? This, of course, is a very personal process, but in my experience it always comes down to spiritual practice. For some that will be yoga or T'ai Chi. For others it will be Buddhist meditation, Kabala, Paganism or Sufism. Still others will find Christian or Jewish forms of prayer and centering helpful. Whatever the form, a daily spiritual practice is the only way I know of to really ground oneself in the truth. One thing is for sure—as long as significant numbers of our community are beating themselves down, our standing up in truth will be very difficult.

In my early conversations with Christian friends, I was very ungrounded. I had not practiced yoga and meditation long enough to really feel confident that I had a right to stand up and be counted as a spiritual seeker. Thus anger and fear were my only response to their evangelizing. As I became more grounded, I no longer needed to yell and scream. I could be calm and state my case while leaving all the drama behind.

The Dalai Lama was once asked how he could be at peace when his home country had been taken from him, his religion had been attacked, and so many of his people had been tortured and killed. Without even a thought, he stated that the Tibetan people had lost so much, why then would he let the Chinese government take his peace too.

If you look at all the great political and spiritual leaders—Gandhi, Martin Luther King, Jr., Nelson Mandela and Oprah Winfrey—they all calmly spoke truth. They all stood tall in their truth and kept their eye on the ball. This is what we must be if we hope to change hearts and minds. Ultimately, changing people's minds about homosexuality is not enough. We need to demonstrate the tolerance, compassion and respect that we ourselves are asking for. Before we can engage conservative Christians in a meaningful discussion about homosexuality, we first need to find our own spiritual grounding.

Once I was walking down the street in San Francisco when a homeless woman accused me of staring at her breasts. She was clearly mentally ill and, I might add, barking up the wrong tree. In any event, I could easily see that she was not well and while I extended her my compassion, I did not share in her delusion. I knew very well that I had not been staring at this woman, and my reaction to her was calm, respectful and compassionate.

Imagine how different my reaction would have been if I had believed her. I would have felt guilty and maybe even made excuses for my alleged behavior. Perhaps I would have reacted with anger or fear. Whatever the case, I would not have been able to help her, and I would have fallen into a tailspin of negative emotions.

I really view conservative Christianity as delusional about certain issues, homosexuality being one of them. There was a time when their attacks would really get me going, and their ability to get such a strong reaction from me had to do with the fact that on some level, I was not spiritually grounded and I knew it. What's worse, my reaction only served to bolster their belief that gay men are crazy.

Now, after years of yoga and meditation, when someone says to me "you're going to go to hell for being gay," I just smile and ask them why they believe that. All the usual Bible verses come up, but now, rather than ranting and raving like a madman, I calmly and quietly explain why their interpretation of anti-gay Bible passages should be reconsidered. Like the farmhand who could sleep when the wind blew because he had prepared, we no longer need to lose our peace of mind when we are attacked because we will have "developed spiritual armor" ahead of time.

Chapter Two

Daily Spiritual Practice

I feel that the essence of spiritual practice is your attitude toward others. When you have a pure, sincere motivation, then you have right attitude toward others based on kindness, compassion, love and respect.

—His Holiness The Dalai Lama

Most of us are familiar with the breakfast cereal "Wheaties" and their marketing campaign of putting famous athletes on the box, the message being that if you want to be strong and athletic, you should eat your Wheaties every day. Well, the same is true about "spiritual athletes." What made people like Martin Luther King, Jr. and Gandhi so powerful? It was eating their spiritual Wheaties every day. For Martin Luther King, Jr., that was Christian prayer. For Gandhi it was Hindu meditation and yoga. The two paths may appear very different, but in reality, spiritual practice is the wind in the sails of all great social revolutionaries. Anyone who has ever been a real social trailblazer has rooted himself or herself deeply in a daily spiritual practice.

Spiritual practice makes us strong and grounds us in our truth. It reminds us daily of what truth is, and in the case of homosexuality, that means remembering that being queer is not a sin or a "biological error"[6] and that queer individuals have a seat at the spiritual table. The problem is, we have been told lies and misinformation about homosexuality and spirituality for so long that on some level, many of us believe these lies and throw the baby out with the baptismal water by avoiding spirituality altogether. A daily spiritual practice is the way in which we reprogram the computer of the mind on a regular basis.

Once I was talking to a queer friend of mine who took a very in-your-face approach to activism. He was yelling at me for not doing more to take a stand against hateful "Christian" ministers. I tried, unsuccessfully, to explain that we are at least as much the problem as the ministers who preach against us. Internalized homophobia results in drug addiction, unhealthy forms of sexual expression, and depression. As long as we try to disarm our external adversaries before first getting our internal demons under control, we cannot make true progress.

This only enraged him further and he wound up storming out of the café we were sitting in. A few years later, he started taking my yoga class. I was surprised to see him as we were not on the best of terms after the café incident, but I was glad he was there. After a few weeks of taking my classes, he approached me and explained that his yoga practice was changing his work as an activist and that he was starting to realize that the more calm and centered he could keep himself, the more persuasive he could be in his activism.

A few years before she died, Mother Theresa opened a center in a poor South American country. Because the

---

[6] "If you're gay or lesbian, it's a biological error that inhibits you from relating normally to the opposite sex." —Dr. Laura Schlesinger

center was so rural, the Vatican had decided to pull the priest out of that village because he was needed elsewhere. This meant that the nuns working for Mother Theresa could not receive the Eucharist (consecrated bread) daily.[7] When Mother Theresa learned of this, she told the Vatican she would be closing the entire place down if they didn't provide a priest. She explained that her sisters could only do the powerful and healing work they were called to do if their own spiritual needs were met first. The Vatican gave in and allowed the priest to stay.

For Mother Theresa and her sisters, the Eucharist is the cornerstone of spiritual practice. For many reading this book, that cornerstone may be something very different. The idea is the same, however: until we heal our own hearts and minds through some form of practice, we will not be able to help others.

On my website, you can find a number of resources for developing a spiritual practice. Whatever your spiritual or religious leanings, I hope you will make both the time and commitment to a daily mindfulness practice such as prayer or meditation. All the facts and skills highlighted in this book will be far less effective unless this one principle is observed.

---

[7] To Roman Catholics, the Eucharist is the most important aspect of spiritual practice. It is believed that it provides a direct link or communion with Jesus.

How To Meditate

The Buddha was once asked which meditation technique was the most effective. The master's response was both simple and profound. "The one you practice." Therefore, start your practice with this simple technique and explore others as well. The important thing is that you get started and that you practice consistently.

Sit in a comfortable upright position. Some people sit cross-legged, and others prefer to kneel. It is also acceptable to sit in a straight-backed chair. Allow your body to relax and take a few deep full breaths to shift into a quiet space.

As you begin to quiet down, focus on the sensation of the breath flowing in and out of the nose where it touches the upper lip. There is no need to change the quality of the breath. Simply watch it move in and out. You will find that the mind will frequently wander. This is natural. Once you notice that the mind has wandered, bring the mind gently back to the breath.

The whole process is one of bringing the mind back to the breath over and over again. Try not to be discouraged by how much the mind will wander. You have been letting your mind wander without discipline for many years. You can't expect it to sit still overnight. Rather than chastising yourself for letting your mind wander, praise yourself for noticing and gently bring it back.

[Excerpt taken from
The Findhorn Book of Meditation
by Darren Main]

Chapter Three

Speaking Truth to Power

"Hope will never be silent."

—Harvey Milk

We need to be very clear about a few things. First, religion is hugely powerful for shaping public opinion, controlling the masses, justifying immoral behavior and, when used properly, for healing. What this means is that those in charge of religion have vast power to affect the way millions live their lives.

Here in the West, we have let Christian fundamentalism run amok with no one standing up to spiritual leaders in the conservative Christian movement and calling their sermons against queer people what they are—hate speech. Certainly Christian ministers and priests are not the only ones who say hateful things about the queer community, but the church is one of the last remaining places where it is deemed socially acceptable to do so. It is no longer OK to yell "faggot" at a guy walking into a gay bar, but it is still very much OK to yell the word "Sodomite"[8] from the pulpit.

Take for example Jerry Falwell's concern about Bill Clinton's lifting the ban on gays in the military because "our poor boys on the front lines will have to face two

---

[8] The word "sodomite" is a favorite in conservative Christian circles. We will explore the origins of this word in Part Two of this book.

different enemies, one from the front and one from the rear."[9] Falwell can get away with this type of statement without social outcry only because he is a minister and talking about gay men. Can you imagine what the public outcry would be if he were to say that African-Americans should not be allowed to serve in the armed forces because "our poor boys on the front lines will have to face two different enemies, one from the front, and another trying to pick his pocket"?

The stereotype that African-Americans are thieves is disgusting and unfortunate, and while some people may still privately hold that ignorant belief, we live in a society that would not condone such statements in our churches.

Why, then, do we just stand by while Falwell and others proclaim the most ignorant and hateful things about queer people? Thousands of gay men have served in the military with honor and distinction. I don't know of any who have raped their fellow soldiers or forced them to participate in any kind of gay sex. That there is no outcry from the masses when statements like this are made—and they are made daily—is truly sad.

To be clear, Falwell has the right to say anything he wants. As an American, his speech, no matter how ignorant and hateful, is and should always be protected. But that doesn't mean we need to sit idly by while he spews slander and lies. Why is it that no one has stood up and called him on this?

Just as Martin Luther King, Jr. stood up and spoke truth to power with regard to black civil rights, we must do the same thing. That said, it is important to follow

---

[9] *Holy War* by Bob Moser. Intelligence Report issue 117, Spring 2005, The Southern Poverty Law Center. www.splcenter.org

King's example of speaking loud and clear but doing so in a way that demonstrates respect for the people with whom we disagree. If we do this, there will come a day, and I believe it will be soon, when it will be just as unacceptable to say hateful, ignorant things about queer men and women as it is to make racial slurs. But that day will only come when we respectfully point out that religion and the Bible are being used as weapons of oppression, rather than as tools for healing.

Come Out, Again

Times sure have changed. When I was a kid, there was nothing worse than being gay. To call someone "gay" on the playground or the school bus was the most effective way to insult and tease, and that was even before any of us knew what "gay" meant. Today, it is trendy to know someone who is gay or lesbian. When my mother started telling her friends that she has a gay son, they were quick to validate her by telling her about all their own gay friends.

This process didn't happen overnight and it didn't happen because of any one event. It happened when queer people decided to come out of the closet, one at a time. It is hard for the younger generations of queer men and women to understand just what a big deal this used to be. Many people lost their families, their jobs and the respect of society as a result of coming out. They came out because they believed in something bigger than themselves—that being queer was as natural to them as being straight was to so many others.

---
[10] http://en.wikipedia.org/wiki/Anti-gay_slogans

Recently I was talking to a 23-year-old gay man who had been out of the closet since he was 15. His parents fully supported him and he even took his boyfriend to the prom. Of course the principal of his high school asked them to leave, but it was a start.

With all this good news, it is easy for us to get lazy and think our work is done. In the early 1990s, the lead singer of the rock band *Skid Row*, Sebastian Bach, wore a shirt on TV that said "AIDS kills fags dead."[10] Such a disgusting shirt is so far out of bounds today it is hard to imagine such a thing ever existed. Something big happened when he wore that shirt, however.

Up until that point, such hateful slurs against queer people were generally accepted. A year prior to that, few would have even noticed he was wearing the shirt. However, the public outrage toward Sebastian Bach was so intense and so fierce that he was forced to apologize publicly for wearing it.

What happened? Why the shift in public opinion? I believe that enough queer people had come out by that point to put a very human face on the issue. Instead of seeing a shirt that said "AIDS kills fags dead," people saw a shirt that might as well have read "AIDS kills your gay (son, roommate, best friend, brother, grandson) dead."

Our work coming out is not done. While it's no longer OK for someone to wear a T-shirt that says hateful things about queer men and women, there is still a place where hate speech toward homosexual and transgender people is very accepted. That place is the pulpit. We need to change this by taking a seat at the table and letting good Christians everywhere know that we are good people

---

[11] In Part Three of this book you can read an essay by my mother, Kathy Ascare, sharing her story. The essay is entitled "Leaving the Church and Finding Love."

who deserve the same rights as everyone else.

I was raised Catholic. When I was growing up, my mother[11] was very devoted to the church and would never question what they taught. Of course, the official teachings of the church are not at all queer-friendly. My mother never questioned this doctrine—not, that is, until I came out.

All of a sudden, the doctrine of the church was not about some depraved, sad, lonely pervert living out in "Frisco."[12] Now the priest was standing there railing against her son, preaching intolerance toward someone whom she knew to be a good person and with whom she was very close.

She had lots of questions for me regarding my spiritual well-being; out of love, she wanted to make sure that her son was not going to hell. After I made the case to her that I am outlining in this book, she found peace.

The last time I spoke with her on this issue she had this to say: "Give me a break, the church wants to judge you for being gay but they cover for child rapists. Hypocrites, that's what they are. I will never put another dime in that collection basket." She hasn't been to church since that scandal broke.

We must not be content to just come out as the trendy and entertaining folks who know the best restaurants and dress really well. Of course those things are important too, but our real work still lies ahead. By changing Christian hearts and minds, we will help to end the hateful preaching that is still very much accepted. Coming

---

[12] In addition to helping my mother question the Catholic stance on homosexuality, I have also taught her not to refer to San Francisco as "Frisco"—further proof that every mother should have at least one queer child.

out—again—is the only way we can do this.

How does one come out *again*? By living a spiritual and moral life that honors and respects people—all people. By being both openly queer or queer-friendly *and* spiritual, and being fearless in our openness about both. By respectfully and thoughtfully disagreeing with religious leaders who still engage in hate speech, and letting people know that one can be spiritual and queer at the same time.

Letting Go of Drama

Drama is a way of life for most Americans. I once heard Fox News host Bill O'Reilly commenting on the success of the Fox News channel. In his view, the channel was doing well because of superior journalism. Others feel Fox is getting good ratings because of their decidedly conservative slant. I, on the other hand, feel that their success is due to the drama.

When I turn on Fox News, more often than not I see people yelling at each other. Maybe it is Sean Hannity yelling at a liberal guest, or O'Reilly hosting guests like Ann Coulter, who is known for making statements that whip up a frenzy of emotion on both the liberal and conservative sides of whatever issue is being discussed.

There is something viscerally satisfying, almost addic-

---

[13] "If gay marriage becomes a reality, then polygamy has to be legalized, because you can't say one alternative group is OK and the other isn't. That's not equal protection under the law. So, if you legalize gay marriage, then polygamy has to be legalized... And if you go to Holland, you'll go to all these other places, you'll see that. The courts there'll let anybody get married to anybody. You want to marry a duck?" —Bill O'Reilly, June 5, 2006, The Radio Factor

tive, about watching all this drama. Seeing a bunch of talking heads duke it out is like getting all juiced on coffee: it feels good and gets you wired. The problem is it never really accomplishes anything. For example, O'Reilly loves the subject of gay marriage and always insists that allowing queer people to marry will open the floodgates, and bestiality and polygamy will soon follow.[13]

This, of course, is an asinine view on the subject and one that any calm and reasonable person could easily tear down, but O'Reilly is nothing if not skilled at getting his guests (not to mention his audience) emotionally wound up. Once this happens, reason and logic are quickly dismissed, and the real issue, gay marriage, is reduced to a screaming match about bestiality.

On a small scale, many of us tend to let the same thing happen in our own personal conversations. It is so much more fun to have a great dramatic debate, to try to pin the other person down and prove that you are right and they are wrong, than to have a calm, reasonable discussion. While this may be satisfying on some level, it will never lead to a meaningful outcome for either person. Thus, resisting the temptation to engage in all the drama will do more to change hearts and minds than just about anything else.

Truth is More Easily Heard When it is Spoken

My former roommate has a beautiful dog, a Weimaraner with silver-grey fur and big green eyes. Her name is Asha, and she was a joy to live with in every way but one: she loves to bark when people come to the door, when large trucks drive by, or when other dogs in the neighborhood bark. Most of the time her barking would only last for a few minutes, but sometimes she would get going like a skipping CD.

Most of the time I could sit at my computer to write and tune her out, but occasionally it would really get under my skin and I would yell at her from my desk. This never worked. Then I would get up and go to the top of the stairs and yell at her. She would keep barking. Finally, I would go downstairs and yell at her. Her response was simply to look at me with her big green eyes and continue barking.

It was actually pretty comedic, and would have been even funnier if I had not been acting so foolishly. There is a saying, "Insanity is making the same mistake over and over and expecting a different result every time." And that was what was happening each time I yelled at Asha for barking.

Dogs have a way of warming your heart if you let them—even when they are barking. As long as I stood there yelling at her she continued to bark. But when I stopped yelling, gave her a hug, and spent some time petting her, the barking stopped, and I was again reminded that calmness and compassion are the answer.

Many conservative Christians are like Asha in that they are very loving, beautiful beings, but every now and then they start barking out phrases like "Adam and Steve" or "It's an abomination." Our natural response is often to get annoyed and yell back, but that only seems to make the barking worse. We can even get right up in their faces, but the barking continues.

My experience is that when you use a compassionate

tone, people respond much better and tend to calm down and listen to what you have to say. If you think back on all the political or religious arguments you have ever had, did you ever get someone to change his or her mind by raising your voice?

It is insanity to keep yelling and think you will win a debate. It will never happen, so learn to keep your tone civil if you truly want to help others open their hearts and minds.

Five Things to Remember about Speaking Truth to Power

1. Stand tall and proud. It is much easier to wrap a noose around a head that is hung in shame.

2. Speak from your peace, not your anger.

3. It is easer to hear a position when the voice offering it is not yelling.

4. Know your facts, and speak them with confidence.

5. Sometimes listening to the point of view of another is the best way to convey your own.

Part Two

The Truth
Shall Set You Free

Blessed are you when men hate you, and ostracize you, and insult you, and scorn your name as evil, for the sake of the Son of Man.

—JESUS OF NAZARETH, LUKE 16:22

Chapter Four

Fear Not the Bible

...The Bible, "The Good Book"– that fascinating anthology of ancient wisdom, history and fable which has for so long been treated as a Sacred Cow that it might well be locked up for a century or two so that men could hear it again with clean ears. There are indeed secrets in the Bible, and some very subversive ones, but they are so muffled up in complications, in archaic symbols and ways of thinking, that Christianity has become incredibly difficult to explain to a modern person."

—ALAN WATTS, ZEN PHILOSOPHER[14]

Know your Facts

A few years ago, Al Gore gave a speech in New York on global warming. Ironically, it was one of the coldest days on record. A politically conservative friend sent me an email calling Gore a "colossal ass" for believing in global warming. His logic was that because it was cold outside, global warming must be a hoax.

There is a colossal ass in this story, but it is not Gore.

---

[14] *The Book on the Taboo Against Knowing Who You Are* by Alan W. Watts Collier books, New York, NY 1966

It is my buddy. There is no debate that the planet is getting warmer, and the temperature on one's thermometer has little to do with how scientists measure climate change.

But while there is no dispute that the planet is getting warmer, there is some disagreement among scientists about how much of that warming is caused by human activity. Most scientists believe that humans are having a huge effect on the warming of the planet; some think we are only a part of the problem. A very small minority believe that human activity has nothing to do with it.

My friend's statement about Gore proved to me that he did not understand the issue and that anything else he might have to say about this issue was likely bogus. Thus, he lost the argument before he even got started.

There are numerous urban legends about the Bible, homosexuality and Christianity on every side. Many Christians like to believe that Jesus denounced homosexuality when the fact is he did not. Many queer and queer-friendly people like to speculate that Jesus and the Apostle John were lovers[15] when there is no basis in fact for such an assumption.

Nothing will kill your argument faster than misstating a fact. Believe me when I tell you that there is no need to go off on wild conspiracy theories about how the church removed all references in the Bible to rainbow flags and pink triangles. There is enough material in the

---

[15] The idea that Jesus and John were lovers is based on a number of passages in the book of John where John refers to himself as "the disciple whom Jesus loved." During the last supper, John even laid with his head in Jesus' lap (John 13:25 and John 21:20.). Arguments have been made on both sides, but the truth is that while Jesus and John were obviously very close, there is no evidence to suggest a romantic or sexual relationship between them.

Bible and enough facts in modern science to make a strong argument that homosexuality is both spiritually and biologically natural, so be sure you don't get caught with bad information.

Don't Be Afraid of the Bible

One of the biggest roadblocks queer and queer-friendly folks have when talking to Christians is that we tend to dismiss the Bible as a witness for our side. Perhaps it is because the Bible has been so effectively used as a weapon by so many "Christians" that we naturally feel repelled by it.

In junior high school, we had a segment in our history class in which we learned about ancient Egypt. According to my teacher, Mrs. Watson, the pharaohs had a tight grip on the masses and kept them intentionally uneducated. Each year, the Nile River would flood and this flooding would provide irrigation for the crops. Thus, the flooding of the river was essential to the survival of the Egyptian peasants.

The pharaohs knew this and would claim to control the river. If the river didn't flood on time, the pharaohs would claim to be displeased with the people. The people, fearing they would not be able to feed their families, would do just about anything to keep the pharaohs happy, which afforded these pharaohs excessive wealth earned on the fear and ignorance of the masses.

The Bible is used as a weapon against many of us, and because we are afraid to really look at it and understand it, hateful "Christian" ministers are able to quote select passages out of context to maintain control over believers and non-believers alike.

In the following chapters, we will be looking at the specific passages in the Bible that are often used to oppress queer men and women, but before we can do that we need to gain a better understanding of the Bible as a whole. The pharaohs realized that knowledge was power, and wanted to keep the people ignorant to serve their own ends. By understanding the Bible and becoming less ignorant of its actual contents, we can take back our power and more effectively educate others.

Understanding the Bible

In the spring of 2004 a movie called *Saved!* opened in theaters. The movie was about a few teens attending a Christian high school. It was a funny exploration of what it means to be Christian. Although it was a dark comedy, it contained a lot of wisdom.

In one scene, one of the girls who had "found Jesus" hurls a Bible at her friend and screams, "I am filled with Christ's love!" Naturally, the audience laughed at this. Their laugher was in part because of the irony involved, but I suspect there was something else that made it comical as well.

While most of us have not had a Bible physically thrown at us, it certainly can feel as if we have. Unfortunately, the Bible has often been used as a weapon rather than a tool to support people in their spiritual growth, and it's no wonder a lot of people would rather eat sand than pick it up and read it. Before we can truly find healing from our Christian pasts and understand what the Bible says about homosexuality, we need to work though our fears and resistances.

I once had a student share with me that she had been raped when she was in college. For years she could not be alone with a man and her sex life disappeared. The mere thought of being with a man brought up fear, anxiety and anger. However, with courage, she was ultimately able to work through that trauma and flourish in her life. She described the process in this way:

"For years I could not even think about dating. On a conscious level I knew rape is an act of violence, not sexuality or love—but on a very deep level I couldn't seem to stop associating the two. With the help of my therapist, I was able to look at that, and I began to realize that the trauma of the rape would never go away unless I found a way to stop associating that traumatic experience with sex in its healthy expression.

"Thankfully, I met Scott. He was so kind and understanding and was willing to take things as slowly as I needed. By exploring my sexuality in the context of a safe and loving relationship, I have moved beyond a lot of that trauma and I'm no longer being victimized by the man who raped me. Scott and I are married now and have a beautiful baby girl."

Her experience is a beautiful example of how the human spirit can overcome trauma with love, patience and willingness to take back our power. Many of us have been violated spiritually by a small yet influential percentage of the Christian religion.

This abuse has nothing to do with Jesus or the Bible. Just as a rapist can use sex as a weapon, the Bible can be used as a weapon by some conservative Christians. Just as a rape victim may simply avoid healthy sexual relationships because of the associations she may hold, we might avoid the Bible. This avoidance, however, only denies us our power.

We need to take back the Bible. We need to look at it for what it is and then make a decision about what role, if any, the Bible will play in our spirituality. The important thing here is that once you look at the Bible in a safe and non-threatening way, the choice will be yours. You will have taken your power back.

Before we can pick up the Bible and read in an effort to dispel religious intolerance toward homosexuality, it is important for us to understand exactly what we are reading. Failure to do this will likely result in our filtering the Bible through old eyes, when what we really need is to see the Bible in a new, more mature and honest light. Thus, understanding the Bible is a necessary first step to interpreting its often cryptic passages about homosexuality.

In this chapter, I want to offer a brief overview of the Bible in an effort to clarify what the Bible is, and more importantly, what it is not.

Bible 101

The Christian Bible is made up of two testaments, the Old and New. Jewish Bibles don't include the New Testament but contain the same basic Old Testament books. The arrangement and translation of Jewish Bibles can be different from Christian editions.

---

[16] The "history" outlined in the Bible is often disputed by historians.

The Old Testament contains thirty-nine books that record the "history"[16] of the Jewish people. The first five books are called The Torah or the Books of Moses. There are also the Books of the Prophets and the Books of Wisdom. The Old Testament was originally handed down as an oral tradition and eventually written in Ancient Hebrew and then translated into modern languages such as English.

The New Testament contains twenty-seven books. These books include the four Gospels, which describe the life and teachings of Jesus; The Acts of the Apostles, which tells about Jesus' followers and the time immediately following Jesus' death; and the Epistles, which are letters written by early Christian leaders such as Saint Paul. The New Testament was written in Greek, translated into Latin and eventually modern languages.

Some Bibles (mainly Roman Catholic) include eleven additional books called the Apocrypha, which are positioned between the Old and New Testaments. The Apocrypha have been a source of tension in Christian communities, with some Christians feeling that these books do not belong in the Bible and others feeling that they are an important part of Scripture. Still others believe that these books are useful, but not the official "Word of God."

The King James Version (KJV) of the Bible is the best-known but the least accurate translation, for reasons that I will explain in Chapter 6. More modern translations such at the New International Version (NIV) or the New Revised Standard Version (NRSV) are more accurate versions and easier to read. In spite of this, some conservative Christians still believe the KJV is the only word of God. We will be discussing the various translations in detail in the following chapters.

As I noted above, the four Gospels tell the story of the life and teachings of Jesus. The first three (Matthew, Mark and Luke) are viewed as "synoptic Gospels" because most scholars believe that these three Gospels share a common yet unknown source and were written around a collection of Jesus' sayings often referred to as the "Q gospel." Although the whereabouts of the Q Gospel is not known, many scholars are convinced that such an account must have existed because of the over-lapping quotes attributed to Jesus in three of the four Gospels.

The fourth, The Gospel of John, is much more poetic and mystical, with its symbolism often misinterpreted. John's gospel is the newest and portrays Jesus in a more divine light, while the synoptic gospels cast Jesus more in the role of a teacher and prophet. Many scholars dismiss much of John's Gospel because it contradicts the three synoptic Gospels in so many ways.

Although Jesus spoke of the apostle Peter[17] as the rock upon which he would build his church, modern Christianity is largely based on the New Testament writings of Saint Paul. He is believed to be the author of quite a number of the Epistles. While his writing has greatly influenced the Christian Church,[18] some feel that his teachings often conflict with the teachings and life example of Jesus.

There are other books written about Jesus that were not included in the Bible, most notably the Gnostic Gospels also known as the Naghamadhi Library. These

---

[17] Matthew 16:18

[18] Another highly influential figure in the Christian church is St. Augustine, who lived around 400 CE. As with Saint Paul, some people feel that Jesus' teachings are at odds with those of St. Augustine'.

were declared heresy and ordered destroyed. Some survived and were found in clay pots in Egypt in 1945.

Navigating the Bible

The Bible is numbered for easy reference. These numbers were not originally part of the Bible, but are now standard in most translations. Whenever I reference the Bible in this book, I will be using this universally accepted system so that you can easily look up the passage for yourself and read the passage in context. Because the numbering system has been applied to almost all modern translations, you can also easily compare various translations.

Reading these numbers is simple. The first part represents the book, the second the chapter, and the third, the verse(s). For example, LK 17:20 would be the Gospel of Luke, Chapter 17, Verse 20.

In addition to a numbering system, section titles have also been added, as well as footnotes. These were not part of the original text, but make for easier reading. Some Bibles even have the words of Jesus in red letters so you can easily find his direct quotes.

The Biblical Slush Pile

A publisher friend once told me that he received hundreds of manuscripts every month, and yet his publishing house only published twenty titles a year. The rest of the manuscripts went into the recycling bin, also known as the "slush pile." Before we go on, I think it's important to address what I call the Biblical slush pile.

Most people don't think much about where the Bible comes from or how it came into being. They just know that they can open a drawer in a hotel room and find a Bible—generally with very thin pages and the word Gideon[19] stamped inside. However, the Bible didn't just magically appear, and the events that the Bible describes didn't take place in a vacuum. Jesus made an impression on many people. Because of this, the Gospel writers were not the only ones to write about him.

The Bible was composed over about a 1,000-year span. Although it is often called the "Good Book," it really should be called the Good *Books* because that is, in fact, what it is. Like the Upanishads that helped to inspire Hinduism and the practice of yoga, the Bible is really a collection of books, each with its own theme and flavor, and in some cases with multiple authors.

This of course raises a very important question: Who decides which books make the final cut and which ones belong in the slush pile? What makes a text *biblical*? This is a question that has been answered by many people over the years with some very different answers. As we have already noted, the Jews don't include the New Testament, and the Roman Catholic Bible includes books called the Apocrypha that most Protestant Bibles don't include. There are other texts that are not included in any mainstream Bible—books such as the Naghamadi Library and the Dead Sea Scrolls. These books have rocked Christian theology, yet they are very misunderstood by both Christians and non-Christians alike.

Before we go on to studying the life and teaching of Jesus as it relates to homosexuality, I think we need to

---

[19] The Gideons are an organization of professional Christian men who, along with their other charitable activities, place Bibles in most hotel rooms.

acknowledge these books. Many lay people are very interested in them. Perhaps it is because they often bolster the belief (one that I share) that Jesus had some very liberal ideas that are not talked about very much in traditional Christian churches.

Another reason we tend to be drawn to these books is because of the "porn principle." This is a term I use for the human attraction to that which is forbidden. When I was young, I was told by my parents that pornography was bad and dirty and that I should never look at it. Consequently, I delighted in sneaking a peek at a *Playboy* when one of the neighborhood kids would swipe one from his father's private stash. Of course I was too young to know what I was looking at, but I knew it must be good if I wasn't supposed to see it.

Because many mainstream Christian churches have denounced these books, many liberal-minded people love to talk about them as if they were the key to unlocking some great conspiracy. People may not know why they like them; they just know they must be good if the Pope says they are bad.

I believe these alternative texts are very valuable and shed a lot of light on the life and teachings of Jesus, but these controversial books need to be properly understood if they are going to be used when we discuss the issues surrounding homosexuality. It is not enough to appreciate something simply because someone else doesn't. So let's briefly look at some of these alternative texts.

Gnostic Gospels

In 1945, a young Egyptian peasant boy found several clay pots containing some old manuscripts. Not knowing what they were, he brought them home. Eventually, they made their way into the hands of some trained scholars who immediately recognized them for what they were: very ancient texts that referred to Jesus. What's more, they were written from a different point of view than the traditional Gospels.

Included in this collection of works are books reported to be authored by Mary Magdalene and The Apostle Thomas (remember doubting Thomas?). Needless to say, these books, if authentic, would raise serious questions about many traditionally held Christian beliefs.

In Mary Magdalene's Gospel, Mary is portrayed as one of Jesus' closest disciples. It is believed by some that she was, in fact, his wife. This casts a dark shadow on the traditional Roman Catholic doctrine that only men can enter the priesthood. It also brings into question the notion that priests should not marry. The idea that Jesus and Mary Magdalene were partnered is not a new one, but a recent flurry of books such as Dan Brown's *DaVinci Code* have pushed the subject into the mass consciousness. [20]

The Gnostic Gospels pose many difficulties in terms of deeply held beliefs about Jesus, his life, and his teachings. Much of what they profess flies in the face of more than 1,500[21] years of tradition. Interestingly, they validate what a lot of non-traditional Christians and mem-

---

[20] The notion that Jesus and Mary were married is not held by most scholars.

[21] Many modern Christian traditions and beliefs have their roots in the council of Nicea which was held in 323 CE. At this council the Nicene Creed, the crux of modern Christianity, was written.

bers of other religions such as Hindus, Muslims and even some Jews have believed about Jesus all along—that he was a great teacher, and perhaps fully realized, but that his message was one of finding one's own connection with God through deep prayer and meditation rather than the worshiping of one being.

So if these documents were so important, why did someone bury them in clay pots? You would think that any documents about a figure who is so central to Western Civilization would be kept well preserved in a museum or something. This brings us back to the idea of a Biblical slush pile.

In the early years of the Catholic Church, when the powers that be were deciding what books would make the final cut, they often declared books that supported Church doctrine as the word of God. Books that didn't fully support the teachings of the Church were called heresy and ordered destroyed. Sadly, many were destroyed, while other manuscripts are rumored to be locked deep inside a Vatican vault somewhere. In any event, some texts were hidden to protect them from the age-old "Christian" tradition of book burning.

So, like the Bible itself, the Gnostic Gospels are the subject of great debate. Some scholars believe them to be as authentic and accurate as the Gospels of the New Testament. Other scholars believe them to be useless and inaccurate. Theologians are similarly divided, which leaves each of us with the very personal question of what place, if any, these books have in our own spiritual life.

Although I personally find the Gnostic Gospels very useful, I have chosen to keep most of my comments in this book confined to the more traditional books of the Bible since it is these books that are used as a weapon against homosexuality. I do, however, suggest that any-one who wants to understand the life and teachings of Jesus investigate the Gnostic Gospels more closely.

The Dead Sea Scrolls

Another thing we need to consider when talking about the Bible is other texts that support or contradict it. Chief among these texts are the Dead Sea Scrolls. They are extensive both in length and in the questions they raise about the very nature of the Bible, especially the nature of the Old Testament, and what Jesus likely believed.

The Dead Sea Scrolls were discovered in 1947, just south of Jericho, by a Bedouin goat herder named Muhammad ed Dip. They were leather-bound scrolls written in both Hebrew and Aramaic.

While they contained a lot of text that was new, they also contained a lot of the content of the Old Testament. The scrolls range greatly in age, with some being the old-est Hebrew texts known (at about 300 BCE) while others are much newer and thought to have been written around the time that Jesus lived. In fact, some of the more modern translations of the Bible such as the NIV have drawn on these scrolls in an effort to be more accu-rate.

In addition to the more familiar books of the Old Testament, there were a number of other scrolls that out-lined the beliefs of a small Jewish sect of mystics called the Esseans. Although there is no conclusive evidence, some scholars speculate that Jesus and John the Baptist were members of this group. If this is true, the Dead Sea

Scrolls would offer a great deal of insight into the life and teachings of Jesus.

Even if Jesus were not an Essean, the Dead Sea Scrolls offer insight into the Hebrew thought and philosophy at the time Jesus was living and teaching as a Jew. Issues about who wrote the Old Testament, the age of these Hebrew texts and the notion that there was a codified Jewish "bible" at the time Jesus was alive are all brought into question.

The Dead Sea Scrolls provide a copious amount of information for scholars to mull over. The scrolls will likely keep academics, theologians and conspiracy theorists busy for many years. Out of all this debate and discussion could arise many challenges to traditional Christian theology and philosophy. As folks seeking to arm ourselves with truth, I believe our goal is to view newly discovered texts such as the Dead Sea Scrolls and the Gnostic Gospels with a neutral eye and an open mind.

In Conclusion

Whether you are a Christian or a Jew, or you practice some other faith, the Bible is a huge part of Western culture. While there is no doubt that the Bible has been used to hurt queer people and other minorities, we can and must take it back. This chapter is only a very brief look at the Bible, so I would recommend that you pursue additional reading that is more exclusively devoted to this important and misunderstood collection of Books. To help get you on your way, I have included a list of suggested reading at the end of this book.

Chapter Five

Literalist vs. Figurative Bible Study

Just because it didn't happen doesn't mean it's not true.

—JOSEPH CAMPBELL

Most of us have had the experience of having someone try to "save" us. You may even have a fundamentalist or Evangelical background yourself. The experience of having someone try to save you is one that can ruin a family function and quite possibly cast a black cloud of guilt over a person's entire life. These sometimes aggressive yet well-meaning Christians will point to a number of Bible verses that would seem to indicate that you had better accept Jesus or you can pack your summer clothes because you'll be looking forward to an eternity in a fiery hell.

There are two ways to read the Bible: literalist and figurative. The people who often "push Jesus" tend to read the Bible from a literalist perspective. For example, when Jesus says, "I am the way the truth and the light. No one comes to the Father except by me," a literalist reader would understand the passage at face value. Thus, if you don't accept Jesus, you don't get to God. To the literalist reader, there is no ambiguity in the statement.

These literalist Christians subscribe to what is commonly call *Biblical inerrancy*—the belief that the Bible is 100% accurate and that anything that casts a shadow of doubt on what the Bible says is flawed, or worse, heresy. We see this reflected in the creationism vs. evolution debate. It doesn't matter how much scientific evidence exists that proves that the earth is much older than the Bible suggests; people who believe that the Bible is without error simply dismiss the evidence, thinking that it is the data or the scientist interpreting that data that is wrong.

In the case of homosexuality we see this over and over again. Every study done on homosexuality has shown that gay men and lesbians can live happy, normal and well-adjusted lives. We can raise healthy, normal and well-adjusted children and contribute greatly to society. Yet, because some Christians perceive that the words of the Bible say homosexuality is a sin, it must be so.

In a world full of uncertainty, I can see why this way of reading the Bible might bring comfort. Having black and white answers to life's many difficulties can bring a certain level of stability. However, this is a false sense of comfort that comes at the price of living in denial, because the Bible itself is full of contradictions. In order to read it literally, one needs to let go of logic.

For example, Jesus says, "I am the way the truth and the light. No one comes to the Father except through me." Then he contradicts himself when a follower who begins to worship him calls him "good teacher" and Jesus replies, "Why do you call me good? Only our Father in Heaven is good." This clearly indicates that reverence and worship should not be directed toward Jesus, but rather toward God. The Bible is riddled with these contradictions, and the only way for someone who takes a literal view of the Bible to resolve them is to shut down the logical mind.

There is a second way to read the Bible that has emerged with the advent of modern science, and this is where the issue of homosexuality can really be resolved. In fact, when viewed through this new lens, many people understandably speculate that Jesus himself would have been very gay-friendly.

This second way of reading the Bible is what has been referred to as figurative reading. To a person reading the Bible through the figurative lens, the Bible's value is not determined by its literal truth. Rather, it is determined by its symbolism and essence—its greater Truth. This frees the reader to maintain a sense of logic, while at the same time growing from the profound wisdom that the New and Old Testament writers have to offer.

In this book we will be exploring the Bible in the figurative sense, and looking at it as it relates to the issue of homosexuality. It is important to note, however, that when you talk to many Christians, they will hold a very literal view of the Bible. Unfortunately, until their perspective on the Bible shifts a bit, it is unlikely they will see eye to eye with you.

I want to make one thing clear, however: I honor the many Christians who have chosen to study the Bible from a literal point of view. I don't often agree with fundamentalist or Evangelical Christians on spiritual issues, and like many, I find constant attempts to save me annoying, but I believe their spiritual path is theirs to walk, not mine to judge.

I once dated a man whose mother was an Evangelical Christian. Her literal view of the Bible led her to a strong belief that homosexuality was sinful. In spite of this, she showed me the utmost kindness, and always treated me as part of the family. While we obviously disagree about homosexuality, I see her as one of the most beautiful examples of what Jesus taught. The fact that she reads the Bible differently than I do in no way lessens the value of her spiritual life. For me to downplay her experience of spirit would be nothing short of spiritual arrogance.

A lot of hurt and suffering has been caused by a literal interpretation of the Bible, and for many of us, much healing needs to be done around this; however, name calling and belittling those who don't share our views will only perpetuate the cycle of ignorance which can only lead to more intolerance.

Jesus vs. Jesus

In 2004 Mel Gibson released his controversial film *The Passion of the Christ*. While it was basically true to the Gospel accounts of Jesus' last hours, it stirred great emotion among many Christians and Jews.

From a traditional Christian point of view, it was a painfully graphic account of the suffering Jesus embraced to free humanity from the bondage of sin. Jews, however, saw the movie as a harsh reminder of the years of persecution inspired by the historically false belief that Jesus was killed by Jews.

This deeply felt conflict was the result of a debate that has been raging among Christians and non-Christians alike: the argument between the Jesus of faith and the Jesus of history. Many Christians have, for thousands of years, believed that the Gospel account of Jesus' life and death was an accurate tale of historical events. Modern scholars have begun the process of painting a very different picture of what likely happened over 2,000 years ago.

This creates a spiritual dilemma for the millions who have built their faith on events they believed to be true. Unlike many Eastern religions such as Hinduism and Buddhism whose followers have always seen the value of books like the Bhagavad Gita as more symbolic than historic, Jews and Christians have always viewed their scriptures as both a source of spiritual guidance and an accurate account of history.

We now know that the events of Jesus' last hours were likely quite different from the way they have been described in the four Gospels. For example, The Jewish high priests are portrayed as demanding that Pontius Pilate, the Roman governor, sentence Jesus to death. After much pleading with the Jewish leaders, when the crowds of Jews gathered outside, he reluctantly sentenced Jesus to death.

Contrast that with the Pilate of history. This Roman governor was known as a brutal dictator who crucified thousands of people, mostly Jews. He was, in many ways, the Hitler of his time. Most historians believe that Pilate would not have given a second thought to executing Jesus and would not have needed the persistent prodding of the Jews to hand down a death sentence.

So which story is true? Was it the Jewish hierarchy that pressed for Jesus' execution, or was it a ruthless dictator who was more than happy to get rid of another Jewish rabbi[22] who was exciting the crowds?

It is not my place to address this issue for Christians who must answer this conflict in their own way. For the purpose of this book, however, it is an issue that must be examined, as the Jesus of history and the Jesus of faith part company in the area of homosexuality. As I write about the events and teachings of Jesus' life with regard to homosexuality, I will do my best to be clear about my source. For the most part, I will be using the books traditionally included in the Christian Bible; however, I will also be drawing on the important work of modern historians as well. I will do my best to make this distinction clear.

One thing that I think is very important to note: just because the account of Jesus' life in the Bible may not be 100% accurate from a historical point of view, this doesn't mean that the stories are not valuable. As Joseph Campbell was always fond of saying, "Just because it didn't happen, doesn't mean it's not true."

Audience

There is another thing we must consider when we read any sacred text: who was the intended audience? When I teach yoga to children, I present it in a very different way than when I am teaching adults. It is not that the essential truth I am trying to convey is any different, but with a different audience I need to change the presentation.

---

[22] During that time, any Jewish teacher was called rabbi. Throughout the Gospels, his followers often refer to Jesus as a rabbi.

The writers of the Bible were no different. Each of them was speaking to a very specific population during a very specific time in history.

For example, the Gospel of Matthew was written for a Jewish audience. He didn't waste time explaining Jewish customs and quoted familiar scripture from the Old Testament without any real explanation. Thus, someone not familiar with Jewish laws and customs of that time would not be able to get a clear picture of what Matthew was trying to express.

Contrast that with the Book of Mark. Mark's audience was clearly Roman. He went into much more detail, describing Jewish laws and customs and even incorporating some Latin into the text. Additionally, he used Roman events to describe time.

This is very important when we consider the issue of homosexuality, because it is not enough simply to look at passages from the Bible and view them with our current understanding of what it means to be queer. To the best of our ability we will need to put ourselves in the position of the people for whom any given passage was intended. To make matters more difficult, books of the Bible were written over a very long period of time and span many generations and cultures. The audience that Jesus spoke to is very different from the one Moses spoke to. All of this needs to be taken into account. Unfortunately many Christians don't take this into account, and as a result their tolerance for queer individuals suffers.

As we discuss passages in the Bible, I will do my best to include some reference to a writer's given audience when I feel the meaning may be taken out of context without clarification.

Hateful vs. Uninformed

One of my best friends, Lance, is an Evangelical Christian. We met as camp counselors in Maine one summer just after college. Each morning, while most of the other counselors were sleeping in, I would get up to practice yoga and meditate. Lance would get up each morning to read the Bible and pray.

I guess it goes without saying that we didn't get along very well. He thought I was going to hell, and I thought he was closed minded and ignorant. Something magical happened that summer though. Being stuck with each other, we were both forced to see beyond the stereotypes we were holding. Ironically, of all the people I lived with that summer, Lance is the only one I have kept in contact with and I consider him a good friend to this day.

The thing about Lance and me is that we still disagree on just about everything when it comes to spirituality. He believes that we are born into sin and that accepting Jesus is the only way to find salvation. I believe we are created perfect and that all of our suffering comes from a false belief about our nature. I believe practices such as yoga, meditation and prayer are tools to help us remember that which can be forgotten but never lost. He believes that accepting Jesus is the only path to God.

I believe the Bible, while a valuable tool, is a product of a very different time and culture and should not be taken literally. Lance, on the other hand, believes the Bible is the perfect word of God and that it is inerrant—that every word it contains should be taken literally. Because of our different interpretations of the Bible, he believes that homosexuality is sinful while I of course do not.

Lance is not a homophobe. He has a number of gay and lesbian friends including me. I believe he is misguided and tell him that often and he tells me the same thing, but he is not anti-gay. In fact, he believes that gays should be allowed to marry and frequently complains when he hears other Christians attack queer men and women because he feels it drives people away from Christ.

Once, a few years ago, Lance and I were giving a joint talk in Louisville, Kentucky. Because Lance is an Evangelical Christian and I am a former Catholic turned yogi, we are, to the casual observer, an odd pair to share a friendship let alone a stage, but there we were. It was Martin Luther King, Jr. weekend, and our purpose for being there was to demonstrate that the tolerance both Jesus and the Reverend King taught was not just a shallow sentiment fit only for greeting cards, but rather something that all true spiritual seekers—especially Christians and yogis—should practice.

During my portion of the talk, I referenced the Bible a number of times in an effort to demonstrate that for all the differences between yoga and traditional Christianity, we had some very important things we could agree on. After each of us had given our presentation, we opened things up to the audience for questions. Most of the questions were respectful and well thought out. But one man in the back of the room stood up. He was shaking with anger and pointing at me.

"How dare you quote the Bible? You are not a Christian. Your sinful lifestyle is evidence of that. This yoga you teach is deceiving people. You have no right to quote from the Bible..." He continued for a minute or two longer.

Lance came to my rescue. "Sir, I read the Bible daily. I am a devout Christian. I have never read anything in the Bible that would justify your behavior right now. In fact, Jesus would never turn someone away."

The man sat down.

When we enter into a discussion about homosexuality with someone who identifies as Christian, it is important to know what kind of Christian he or she is. Most are like Lance—good people with strong personal beliefs. They are not homophobic and have no interest in hurting or oppressing anyone.

Unfortunately there are other "Christians" who are very hateful and regularly attack queer people. They believe we should have limited rights, that we should be kept away from children and that we are the cause of everything bad in society. This is where the term homophobic would be more accurate.

With someone like Lance, a discussion about homosexuality is usually productive and will often lead to a better mutual understanding. The more hateful "Christians" are probably not ready for such a meaningful discussion and are better left alone until they are ready. Trying to respectfully discuss any issue with a person blinded by hate is like "throwing pearls to pigs."[23]

---

[23] "Do not give dogs what is sacred; do not throw your pearls to pigs. If you do, they may trample them under their feet, and then turn and tear you to pieces." Matthew 7:6

Chapter Six

Knocking King James off His Throne

He who reads the Bible in translation is like a
man who kisses his bride through a veil.
—HAYYIM NACHMAN BIALIK

As I mentioned already, there are different versions of
the Bible for Catholics, Jews and other Christian denominations. Knowing which Bible to read is confusing
enough, but that's only the beginning. Most versions
also have multiple translations. The most commonly
known English translation is the King James Version
(KJV). This is the translation that cursed us with what I
call "Bible Speak." Every other word is thee or thou, and
reading it makes Shakespeare look like cotton candy.

Around 1604, the Puritans in England began to peti-
tion King James on a number of religious issues including an officially sanctioned Bible. The king agreed and
commissioned a new Bible to be translated. It was com-
pleted around 1611.

The King James Version is often criticized by scholars
and contemporary Christians. However, King James did
contribute something important: the King James Bible
became widely available to scholars and laypeople alike.
Although seriously flawed, the KJV helped take the Bible

out of the guarded clutches of a few and furthered the cause of making it accessible to the masses.

Today there are over 100 versions of the Bible in more than 400 languages. While more current translations of the Bible are considered more accurate[24] than the King James Version, all translations are flawed by virtue of the translation process. When you consider the amount of information that gets lost in translation and the massive obstacles this presents, it is a great wonder that we can understand the Bible at all.

Take the New Testament for example. People who never personally met Jesus wrote each of the four Gospels. In fact most modern scholars believe the earliest Gospel was written no sooner than thirty years after Jesus' crucifixion[25]. Now, I don't know about you, but I was led to believe that Matthew, Mark, Luke and John were sitting at Jesus' sandal-clad feet, busily writing down every word Jesus said. The truth is the four Gospels were written by people who never even met Jesus, and they tailored their accounts to the audience they were addressing.

It gets even trickier. The original Gospels were written in Ancient Greek. But Jesus didn't speak Greek, he spoke Ancient Aramaic. What this means is that not only did the scribes of the New Testament not know Jesus personally, but they were translating it from the words he spoke in one language to a completely different language.

---

[24] A small yet vocal number of conservative Christians believe that the KJV is the only legitimate English version of the Bible. Their beliefs are more theological than academic, however.

[25] Some conservative scholars date the Gospels earlier but even their dates place the earliest Gospels years after Jesus' death.

You can see why this is a problem. This is like playing telephone—that game in which kids pass a phrase from one person to the next, only to have the phrase jumbled beyond recognition by the end of the line. Now imagine what you would have if the phrase were translated into a new language with every third person.

You can already see how staggeringly difficult this is, and there is yet another problem to consider. The Old Testament was written in ancient Hebrew.[26] The Ancient Jews had a mostly oral tradition for hundreds of years, and the stories of King David, Adam and Eve, and Abraham were not written down until hundreds of years after the events in the Old Testament were alleged to have happened.

So not only do translators have to deal with the translation from one language to another, they also have to deal with multiple languages, multiple cultures, and an oral tradition from which most of these texts originated.

My reason for exploring the difficulties with translation is to set the stage for a deeper study of the Bible. Once we understand what we are reading, we can take a more balanced and honest approach to it. The first step in understanding the Bible is to understand that it is not perfect. Once we acknowledge this, we can begin to mine its depths for a much deeper Truth, a Truth that I believe holds freedom from homophobia and religious intolerance.

For the purposes of this book, I have chosen to quote primarily from the New International Version or NIV.

---

[26] Ancient Hebrew is related to but different from the Modern Hebrew that is spoken in Israel today.

[27] www.gospelcom.net

The NIV was translated in the 1970s, making it a much more modern translation. According to the official NIV website,[27] the NIV is "a completely new translation of the Holy Bible made by over a hundred scholars working directly from the best available Hebrew, Aramaic and Greek texts." The site goes on to say, "The fact that participants from the United States, Great Britain, Canada, Australia and New Zealand worked together gave the project its international scope. That they were from many denominations—including Anglican, Assemblies of God, Baptist, Brethren, Christian Reformed, Church of Christ, Evangelical Free, Lutheran, Mennonite, Methodist, Nazarene, Presbyterian, Wesleyan and other churches—helped to safeguard the translation from sectarian bias."

Many of the other versions of the Bible were translated by people strictly of one faith or another. This is not to say their intentions were not good; it is simply a matter of human nature to slant things to one's own point of view. Because the NIV was translated by a panel of scholars from a variety of perspectives, I give it a bit more credence. I am still waiting to see a gay scholar on the panel, but until then, I think the NIV team did an adequate job of representing the ancient Greek and Hebrew texts.

Translation and Homosexuality

Homosexuality as we know it today did not exist in Biblical times. Ancient Jews were aware of same-sex acts to be sure, but the notion that two men or two women would partner in the same way a husband and wife would was completely foreign to that culture. Given all the recent press on issues such as gay marriage and gays in the military, it is hard to imagine a time before Will & Grace.[28]

To understand the difference between Biblical references to same-sex acts and a modern concept of homosexuality, we need to be clear about the different definition of romantic relationships at that time. In our culture we tend to take a "Meg Ryan" approach to romance. Really, to understand this view of romance all you need to do is rent a Meg Ryan movie.

The movie will involve love at first sight, a problem or conflict to be overcome, maybe a funny scene involving a faked orgasm in a crowded place, and the couple ultimately getting together and living happily ever after. Now, some (like myself) might argue that this model is insipid and unrealistic, but for better or worse, this is how our culture views heterosexual relationships and to a large degree same-sex relationships as well.

During Biblical times, Meg Ryan would not have fit in very well. In the view of ancient Jewish culture, a marriage had little to do with love and was more of a business arrangement (known as betrothal) with procreation being the primary function. Thus we see people being stoned for adultery and women being shamed for not being able to bear children. Love and mutual respect was something that, while present and important, was not really the central issue in marital partnerships, nor was sexual preference. It was all about making babies, and if you were not particularly in love or attracted to your

---

[28] *Will & Grace* was a popular sitcom about a gay man, Will, and his best friend Grace, a straight woman. The show marked a turning point in popular culture in that homosexuality was not portrayed as controversial or edgy in the way it had been in previous gay-themed shows such as *Ellen*.

partner, then you simply had to deal with it. Almost all men and women of childbearing age were married.

The notion that two men could meet, fall in love and live happily ever after with two cats and a charge account at Pottery Barn, or two women could fall in love and decide to move in together after the second date, simply didn't exist. Some men and women clearly would have had same-sex attractions, but they would have had to act on these attractions outside of their marriages.

In truth, the study of homosexuality is only about 100 years old, and thus scholars such as Daniel A. Helminiak refer to biblical references to same-sex acts as "homogenitality."[29] Even the word homosexual didn't appear in a Bible until 1946 when the Revised Standard Version (RSV) began translating a variety of Greek and Hebrew words as "homosexual."

Many translations of the Bible use the word "sodomy" or "sodomite" when referring to same-sex acts, but here too we find a gross mistranslation. While the word sodomy in modern English has come to be associated with homosexuality in general and anal sex in particular, there is no such word in the Bible.

The word sodomy is derived from the name of the infamous Biblical town of Sodom that God ultimately destroyed for its sins. Many have argued that the sin of Sodom was homosexuality, but as we shall see shortly, the sins of Sodom had little to do with sex—gay or straight. The word sodomite, then, rather than referring to gay or anal sex, is more properly a reference to one who lived in the city of Sodom in the same way we would refer to someone from New York as a New Yorker.

---

[29] *What the Bible Really Says about Homosexuality,* Daniel A. Helminiak, PhD, p. 39

Chapter Seven

The Purity Laws

The Bible contains six admonishments to homosexuals and 362 admonishments to heterosexuals. That doesn't mean that God doesn't love heterosexuals. It's just that they need more supervision.

—LYNN LAVNER

In the last chapter, we discussed the importance of knowing the audience to which a biblical writer was speaking, and nowhere is this more important than in regard to the Purity Laws of the Old Testament, upon which many Christians base their intolerant views of homosexuality. Before we can really look at what the Purity Laws say about homosexuality, we need to become clear about the audience to which they were directed and why.

Because we live in a Jeffersonian democracy, the notion of separation of church and state is a principle we are born into. Sure, there are disagreements about where that line should be drawn, giving rise to issues such as prayer in public schools, but we all agree that there is a line between the two. We can go to a church, synagogue or mosque for spiritual guidance and community, and we rely on the state and federal governments to address issues such as health care, defense, education and criminal justice.

When you walk into a restaurant, you know it is regulated by the state health code. If you want to know if a drug is safe and effective, you can turn to the Food and Drug Administration, and if you fear that Canada will someday invade our country, you count on the U.S. military to defend us. We can have all sorts of political debates about how best to accomplish these goals and whether or not these agencies are doing their jobs in an effective way, but we all agree that the execution of these very important tasks is not the responsibility of the church.

This was not the case in early Judaism—quite the opposite was true. There was no line between church and state. Everything was regulated and controlled by the religious leaders of the time. The legal system, health code and just about every other facet of daily life we associate with a democratic government was regulated by the church. Thus, the Old Testament is not just a collection of books that deal solely with issues of spirituality; the books of the Old Testament address every facet of Jewish society at the time.

The Hebrew Purity Laws, which make up a significant portion of the Old Testament, are really like a combination of state health code and FDA regulations with a little criminal justice and civil law thrown in. Many modern-day Jews base Kosher dietary guidelines on some of these Purity Laws as many of these laws have to do with diet and cleanliness. For example, a woman on her menstrual cycle was considered to be unclean; there were strict rules about what women could and could not do and when it was safe to touch a woman who was on her cycle.

Of course, today most of these laws seem very outdated. With modern science and medicine, we now know that women on their cycle are not in fact unclean, and that stoning a woman to death for touching someone while on her cycle is a tad excessive.

Even before modern advancements in science and medicine, people had started to question many of the Purity Laws. Jesus himself did this often by eating without first ritually washing his hands,[30] touching women on their cycle[31] and spending time with lepers[32]. Not only did he break these laws openly, but he criticized the Scribes and Pharisees who clung to the letter of the law without following the spirit behind the laws.

Several of the verses that Christians quote in their efforts to denounce homosexuality come from the book of Leviticus and are part of the Purity Laws of that time, and although most of the other Purity Laws were dismissed by even the most conservative Christians long ago, they still cling to the ones that denounce homosexuality as an "abomination."

Joe Decker and Rayland Sanders host the very funny website GodHatesShrimp.com, which is a parody on this very subject. Based on the hate-filled website of The Rev. Phelps, GodHatesFags.com, their website points out just how silly people like Phelps really are in their selective interpretation of scripture. In effect, what they are saying is that trying to use the Purity Laws to condemn homosexuality makes about as much sense as using the

---

[30] Matthew 15:2

[31] Matthew 9:20

[32] Matthew 8:2, 26:6, Mark 1:40, 14:30

same laws to condemn people for eating shellfish—
something expressly forbidden in the Purity Laws.

Again, it is essential that I stress that virtually no person of faith in the modern world, Christian or Jew, fol-
lows these laws though some Jews still observe a few of
the dietary laws.

For the most part, these laws are seen as a product of
the time and culture in which they were written, and
irrelevant to a modern civilized society. Contemporary
science and the rule of law have made them obviously
outdated.

For example, to name just a few, the laws endorse slavery (Lev 25:44), forbid hair cuts, shaving and getting tat-
toos (Lev 19:27-28), demand a child be executed for
speaking out against his or her parents (Lev 20:9), forbid
intercourse with a woman on her menstrual cycle (Lev
18:19) and demand the execution of anyone guilty of
adultery (Lev 20:10).

As crazy as all that sounds, some Christians still hold
tightly to two such laws in the book of Leviticus that
address the issue of homosexuality. Take the issue of
slavery. Aside from a few crazy folks in northern Idaho,
no one believes slavery is acceptable. It is one of the
greatest embarrassments in human history and no one,
Christian or otherwise, disputes that. Yet many of the
Old Testament laws and even some passages from the
New Testament were invoked to justify slavery. Regard
this passage from Jefferson Davis' inaugural address as
President of the Confederate States:[33]

> "[Slavery] was established by decree of Almighty
> God...it is sanctioned in the Bible, in both

---

[33] Jefferson Davis, "Inaugural Address as Provisional President of the
Confederacy," Montgomery, AL, Feb. 18, 1861, Confederate States of
America. Congressional Journal, 1:64-66. www.religioustolerance.org

> Testaments, from Genesis to Revelation... it has
> existed in all ages, has been found among the
> people of the highest civilization, and in nations of
> the highest proficiency in the arts."

The Purity Laws are found throughout the Old
Testament but the vast majority are located in the book
of Leviticus. With the exception of the story of Sodom
that we will discuss in the next chapter, there are only
two short passages denouncing homosexuality in the
Old Testament and both are from Leviticus. So what does
the book of Leviticus say about homosexuality?

> Do not lie with a man as one lies with a woman; that
> is **detestable**.—Leviticus 18:21

> If a man lies with a man as one lies with a woman,
> both of them have done what is **detestable**. They
> must be put to death; their blood will be on their
> own heads. —Leviticus 20:13

I have emphasized the word "detestable" because it is
so important to the passage. While the above passages
come from the New International Version, the King
James Version uses the word "abomination." I know,
detestable, *abomination*, what's the difference, right?
Both words are used to describe a sex act as unsavory.
A closer look at the Hebrew translation, however, reveals
something interesting.

The Hebrew word that is translated above as
"detestable" and "abomination" is *toevah*. The literal
meaning of *toevah* is "unclean."[34] Now, this puts an
entirely different spin on the passage. When you read
words like "detestable" and "abomination," images
come to mind of a God with a long white beard looking

---

[34] *What the Bible Really Says about Homosexuality*, Daniel A. Helminiak,
Ph.D, pp. 57-58, 64

down from the heavens and trying to fight back dry heaves because he is so revolted by seeing two men or two women making love. However, the literal translation of "unclean," although very judgmental, fits more with many of the other Purity Laws. Contrast that with the word in Hebrew for sin or spiritually immoral, *zimah*. Had the Old Testament writers wanted to convey that homosexuality is immoral they would have used the word *zimah* rather than *toevah*.

Consider the difference between a man killing a person and a cook not washing his hands before returning to work after using the bathroom. Both acts are illegal, but for very different reasons. Murdering someone is morally wrong and thus we have laws against it. Not washing one's hands is not about morality per se, but rather about what our society considers clean. For the most part, every society considers murder immoral or *zimah*. What is considered unclean or *toevah* varies from culture to culture.

It is also important to point out that the above passages address men only. Any lesbians reading this book should not get too excited just yet. While most of the anti-gay passages in the Bible denounce sex between men, this has more to do with the fact that women were held in such low regard at the time that their sexuality beyond procreation was rarely acknowledged. The word for woman in Hebrew is *naqeba* which literally means "orifice bearer."—hardly a feminist description.

While using the word *toevah* to describe sex between two men isn't very flattering, as we discussed in the previous chapter, knowing the audience is key. At the time the book of Leviticus was authored, procreation was something of a mystery. Modern science would not arrive for thousands of years, and the common belief was that a man's sperm or "seed" was planted in the womb of a woman. The resulting pregnancy was not viewed as the union of a sperm and an egg, but rather as a man's seed growing inside a woman. Thus the woman was seen as little more than an incubator.

A man's semen was also viewed as being limited in supply. It was thought that every drop should be used for the purpose of procreation; to waste it in acts such as masturbation or gay sex was a crime against the Jewish society. That seed was to be growing in a womb. Of course we know now that men continue to produce sperm throughout life, and semen is hardly in short supply.

Lastly, let us again consider the audience. It is exceedingly important to remember that our view of gay and lesbian relationships is something that simply didn't exist at the time the stories and laws in the Old Testament originated. Again, this is not to say that gay sex was not around or that same-sex relationships were unheard of,[35] but Jewish culture at that time was vastly different than the popular Charlton Heston movies of the 1960s would have you believe. The Jewish tribes were nomadic and traveled from place to place. It was a dangerous time, when such traveling often resulted in short lifespans—bad news for a small community trying to survive as a people. Thus every womb was seen as wasted if it was not perpetually pregnant, and every man was seen as a source of "seed" that should keep his wife pregnant as often as possible. It is for this reason there was no greater shame in ancient Jewish culture than that of a woman unable to bear children.[36]

---

[35] As we will discuss later in this book, gay relationships in the Bible are well documented.

This may sound crude, and in today's world of over-population it is, but at that time survival of the tribe was paramount. Falling in love, getting married and living happily ever after was not a goal for men and women, and finding a same-sex life partner was not even on the radar. Thus the Purity Laws dealing with sexuality usually reflected these beliefs around procreation.

To a certain extent many of these laws made sense at the time, yet cultures change as does our understanding of the world. As this happens, we need to re-examine social mores such as those outlined in Leviticus and other Old Testament books. As we saw earlier, Jesus himself was continually doing this and angering the establishment at every turn. By questioning the Purity Laws, Jesus set himself apart from the religious fanatics of his time, and I have no doubt that if he were alive today, he would be doing the exact same thing with regard to the two passages in the book of Leviticus concerning homosexuality.

---

[36] Of course we now know that difficulties in reproduction can also be attributed to the man, but at that time problems were usually blamed on the woman.

Chapter Eight

The Sins of Sodom

If God doesn't destroy Hollywood Boulevard, he owes Sodom and Gomorrah an apology.

—JAY LENO

There is perhaps no narrative from the Bible more cited with regard to homosexuality than that of Sodom. Even the term sodomy is rooted in this Biblical story. Many conservative Christians would have us believe Sodom was an ancient town destroyed by God for the sin of homosexuality. A close look at this story, however, paints a very different picture of why God might be angry, and it has nothing to do with homosexual relationships.

Before we get into the finer points of the story with regard to homosexuality, let's take a look at a few of the highlights. The hero is a man named Lot, who is a very righteous man in good favor with God. Lot and his family lived in the town of Sodom. Sodom was the Las Vegas of its time, and the locals liked debauchery. A great war had just ended, and morality was the last thing on people's minds. Thus the town had a reputation for loose morals and rowdy behavior. Unlike much of Jewish culture, a rather low value was placed on the whole family ethic of the time—think Mardi Gras. This behavior angered God, and he decided to do something about it. So he sent two angels in human form to warn Lot that God was not happy with the free-for-all happening in Sodom, and that very bad things lay in store if the free-for-all was not brought under control.

The plot thickened when a group of rowdy men heard that these two visitors were in town, and they decided it would be fun to gang rape them. We are not talking about a love story on par with *Brokeback Mountain* or an evening of love-making. We are not even talking about recreational sex, a one-night stand or a consensual orgy—we are talking about rape.

So the mob showed up at Lot's home and Lot pleaded with them not to violate the travelers. You see, while much has changed over the past three thousand years or so, this principle has remained largely consistent—rape is not a nice thing to do to someone, and it is certainly not considered hospitable.

Most can agree that rape is immoral and our hero, Lot, being righteous, thought so too. But Lot's issue with rape was not for the reasons you might expect. So Lot continued to beg and plead with the men to convince them that what they wanted to do—rape his guests—was wrong. He even went so far as to offer the men his two virgin daughters to gang rape instead.

Unfortunately, the prospect of the two virgin daughters didn't appease the mob. They were hell-bent on forcing themselves onto Lot's guests and it became clear that Lot, his family and the two angels needed to make a swift escape. The angels helped Lot and his family escape before God took the city and everyone in it out with a rain of fire from heaven.[37] The angels also instructed Lot and his family not to look back as they left the city. His wife couldn't resist and was turned into a pillar of salt when she looked over her shoulder.

This gang of wild men was guilty of one crime according to Jewish law at that time, and it had nothing to do with homosexual love. The law had to do with hospitality. Because travel was so difficult at the time, there were very strong customs about how to treat travelers. Moving from town to town meant risking your life, so when you got to your destination it was essential that you had a safe place to stay. While this may seem odd to us in the age of cheap hotel chains, it was very much the reality of the day.

A reflection of this idea can be seen in Jesus' birth narrative in which Mary and Joseph are forced to stay in a stable on the night Jesus was born. To a traveling Jew, few things were a bigger insult than to enter a town and be treated without hospitality. Jewish custom put an exceedingly high value on welcoming travelers as if they were family.

Obviously this gang of men was not being hospitable, which leads us to a second very important point. Women, as I have noted, were second-class citizens and considered the property of their husbands or fathers. Forcing a man to take the female role in a sex act was about the most degrading thing you could do, the height of insult.[38]

---

[37] God, at least in the Old Testament, is very creative in the ways in which he can smite sinners; swarms of locusts, killing off firstborn children, floods, fire falling from the sky, and famines, just to name just a few.

[38] In many Middle Eastern cultures, this is still true today. In fact, this is one of the reasons there was such outrage over the abuses at Abu Gharib.

A third point needs to be made about this story. It shouldn't need to be made, but since so many people seem to overlook this tiny detail when condemning homosexuality, I think it is essential to point this out. Lot, the hero of the story, offered his virgin daughters to the mob for a gang rape. This is hardly a story I would point to as a way to set my moral compass with regard to sexuality.

Although Lot was considered a righteous man in the story, he was not what we could call the model father. After his wife had turned to salt, he lived in a cave with his daughters. After having too much wine, he and his daughters had sex, which resulted in their becoming pregnant (Genesis 19:30-36).

I will be the first to admit that the Bible leaves a lot of room for different interpretations, and certainly different people can read the same passage and arrive at divergent opinions. But I can't for the life of me understand how someone can get an anti-gay message from this story. Even if we read the story from a literal point of view, the best we can really come up with is that it is wrong to gang rape adult men, but it is OK for a father to turn his virgin daughters over to the same fate.

When I have talked to Christian friends about this, they never have a real answer. Most open-minded and intellectually honest Christians will admit that the story of Sodom's destruction had nothing to do with gay sex, or sex at all for that matter. It had to do with a lack of hospitality that found its expression in gang rape and violence.

From the Source

The two angels arrived at Sodom in the evening, and Lot was sitting in the gateway of the city. When he saw them, he got up to meet them and bowed down with his face to the ground. "My lords," he said, "please turn aside to your servant's house. You can wash your feet and spend the night and then go on your way early in the morning."

"No," they answered, "we will spend the night in the square."

But he insisted so strongly that they did go with him and entered his house. He prepared a meal for them, baking bread without yeast, and they ate. Before they had gone to bed, all the men from every part of the city of Sodom—both young and old—surrounded the house. They called to Lot, "Where are the men who came to you tonight? Bring them out to us so that we can have sex with them."

Lot went outside to meet them and shut the door behind him and said, "No, my friends. Don't do this wicked thing. Look, I have two daughters who have never slept with a man. Let me bring them out to you, and you can do what you like with them. But don't do anything to these men, for they have come under the protection of my roof."

"Get out of our way," they replied. And they said, "This fellow came here as an alien, and now he wants to play the judge! We'll treat you worse than them." They kept bringing pressure on Lot and moved forward to break down the door.

But the men inside reached out and pulled Lot back into the house and shut the door. Then they struck the men who were at the door of the house, young and old, with blindness so that they could not find the door.

The two men said to Lot, "Do you have anyone else here—sons-in-law, sons or daughters, or anyone else in the city who belongs to you? Get them out of here, because we are going to destroy this place. The outcry to the LORD against its people is so great that he has sent us to destroy it."

So Lot went out and spoke to his sons-in-law, who were pledged to marry his daughters. He said, "Hurry and get out of this place, because the LORD is about to destroy the city!" But his sons-in-law thought he was joking.

With the coming of dawn, the angels urged Lot, saying, "Hurry! Take your wife and your two daughters who are here, or you will be swept away when the city is punished."

When he hesitated, the men grasped his hand and the hands of his wife and of his two daughters and led them safely out of the city, for the LORD was merciful to them. As soon as they had brought them out, one of them said, "Flee for your lives! Don't look back, and don't stop anywhere in the plain! Flee to the mountains or you will be swept away!"

But Lot said to them, "No, my lords, please! Your servant has found favor in your eyes, and you have shown great kindness to me in sparing my life. But I can't flee to the mountains; this disaster will overtake me, and I'll die. Look, here is a town near enough to run to, and it is small. Let me flee to it—it is very small, isn't it? Then my life will be spared."

He said to him, "Very well, I will grant this request too; I will not overthrow the town you speak of. But flee there quickly, because I cannot do anything until you reach it." (That is why the town was called Zoar.)

By the time Lot reached Zoar, the sun had risen over the land. Then the LORD rained down burning sulfur on Sodom and Gomorrah—from the LORD out of the heavens. Thus he overthrew those cities and the entire plain, including all those living in the cities—and also the vegetation in the land. But Lot's wife looked back, and she became a pillar of salt.

—Genesis 19:1-26

Chapter Nine

Saint Paul's View of Homosexuality

And if I dole out all my goods, and if I deliver my body that I may boast, but have not love, nothing I am profited. Love never falls in ruins; but whether prophecies, they will be abolished; or tongues, they will cease; or knowledge, it will be superseded.

—SAINT PAUL

Before we dig into the New Testament references to homosexuality, it would be a good idea to understand one of the central figures in the New Testament. As many as 14 of the Epistles (or Letters) in the New Testament are attributed to Paul, and it is here that we find references to homosexuality in the New Testament.

Paul never knew Jesus and in fact started his career persecuting Jesus' early followers in the years just after his crucifixion. Paul was born in Tarsus, Turkey. His original name was Saul. After spending the first part of his life persecuting early Christians such as Saint Stephen,[38] he had a life-changing experience while traveling on the road to Damascus. According to scripture, Jesus spoke to him saying, "Saul, Saul, why do you persecute me?",[39] after which he fell to the ground blinded. He was then

---

[38] Acts 8:1-3

[39] Acts 26:14

taken to Damascus where he was healed and baptized by an early Christian named Ananias and with that baptism took on the name Paul.

After his conversion, Paul began to preach. What set Paul apart from most in the early church was his audience. While most early Christians and even Jesus himself were largely interested in preaching to fellow Jews, Paul went out and started to convert Gentiles (non-Jews). This fact will become very important as we start to look at his teachings on homosexuality.

While Jesus was very much aware of the Gentiles around him and even healed them from time to time, he never tried to convert them. It is also clear that Jesus was not out to start his own religion. He was Hebrew, and sought only to clarify what he viewed as a misuse, abuse even, of the Torah by the Scribes and Pharisees. At no point did he try to convert or even condemn the Romans and other Gentiles around him.

Paul's worldview was decidedly more broad than that of the other New Testament writers and of Jesus himself. He traveled extensively. In non-Jews he saw a whole new market, so to speak, and he devoted much of his time to preaching to the Gentiles. In much of his writing, he sought to highlight the differences between Roman culture and behavior and that of the newly forming Christian Church.

In many ways, Paul was the first Born Again or Evangelical Christian. His rebirth on the road to Damascus, and his subsequent evangelizing or preaching to Gentiles, make him stand out in the early church.

This was a difficult time for all the members of the early Christian movement in general. What did it mean to be Christian? A seemingly simple question with anything but simple answers. Were early Christians a sect of Judaism, or were they their own religion? Should Gentiles be accepted into this new religion, and if so should they adopt Jewish customs such as circumcision? Clearly the Torah and the Books of the Old Testament prophets were important to early Christians, but if Jesus had indeed fulfilled the Hebrew scriptures, then what role would these scriptures play? For example, what role, if any, would the Purity Laws play in the lives of Christians? The early church was a time of sorting out what it meant to be a follower of Jesus and for whom his message was intended.

Paul was clearly of the belief that Jesus' message, at least as he understood it, was open to Jews and Gentiles alike. Paul would frequently try to define what it meant to be a Christian by highlighting the differences between the Christian Jews and the Romans. One of the ways in which he did this was by addressing the Roman cultural norms about sexuality in general and same-sex relationships in particular. Now, I use the term "same-sex relationships" very loosely because the relationships which so offended Paul were very different than the typical gay or lesbian relationships we see in modern society.

From The Source

Therefore God gave them over in the sinful desires of their hearts to sexual impurity for the degrading of their bodies with one another. They exchanged the truth about God for a lie, and worshipped and served created things rather than the Creator—who is forever praised. Amen. Because of this, God gave them over to shameful lusts. Even their women exchanged natural sexual relations for unnatural ones. In the same way the men also abandoned natural relations with women and were inflamed with lust for one another. Men committed shameful acts with other men, and received in themselves the due penalty for their error.

—Romans 1:24-27

Do you not know that the wicked will not inherit the kingdom of God? Do not be deceived: Neither the sexually immoral nor idolaters nor adulterers nor male prostitutes nor homosexual offenders*.

—1 Corinthians 6:9

. . .for adulterers and perverts, for slave traders and liars and perjurers—and for whatever else is contrary to the sound doctrine.

—1 Timothy 1:10

(*A note on "Homosexual offenders:" this is the New International Version of the Bible's translation of the Greek word *arsenokoitai*. There are other versions of the Bible that translate it differently. While there is much debate about Paul's use of this word, scholars agree that it is not an easily translated word, as is noted below.)

Before we dig into Paul's statements about homosexuality, it is important to know where he was coming from in general. According to Bishop John Shelby Spong, Paul did not view homosexual acts as a sin; rather, he viewed homosexual acts as punishment.[40]

---

[40] *Living in Sin? A Bishop Rethinks Human Sexuality* by John Shelby Spong, pp. 149-150

Don't get me wrong, Paul was certainly not an early member of PFLAG.[41] A simple analogy would be gluttony, one of the seven deadly sins. Just as the result of gluttony would likely be obesity, Paul seemed to view homosexuality as the logical consequence of lust, another of the seven deadly sins.

This may not seem like a huge distinction, but in some key ways it is exceedingly important. Consider this: just because a person has a large or round body doesn't mean he is gluttonous. Likewise, just because someone is attracted to a member of the same sex and forms a romantic relationship doesn't mean he or she is guilty of lust. Again, this is not to imply that Paul was a fan of gay relationships, but, according to Bishop Spong, he likely viewed homosexuality as the symptom, not the disease.

So what did the Roman brand of homosexuality that so offended Paul look like? For starters, Roman notions of homosexuality were often associated with ritual and many of the acts Paul describes are not what we in the modern world would think of as a gay relationship. Same-sex prostitution, sexual slavery, and an older man having a younger male lover were all very common in Roman culture, and certainly frowned upon by Jews and Christians of that time in much the same way that such relationships would not be accepted in most cultures today. In fact, Paul's word choice in the original Greek is *arsenokoitai*[42] which properly translates as "perverts" or "male prostitutes."[43]

When viewed in this light, one can easily see a distinction between the same-sex sexual acts to which Paul

---

[41] Parents and Friends of Lesbians and Gays

[42] 1 Timothy 1:10

[43] *What the Bible Really Says about Homosexuality,* Daniel A. Helminiak, PhD, p. 108

referred, and what today we conventionally think of as a gay or lesbian relationship. Certainly male prostitutes still exist, and there are some gay men and lesbians who might be considered perverted, just as there are heterosexual prostitutes and straight forms of perversion. Paul would no doubt find both offensive. What is in question is what Paul would have to say about loving relationships between two women or two men.

To be honest, I don't know how Paul would feel about modern gay and lesbian relationships, and if conservative Christians were being honest, they would have to admit as much as well. What I can say with certainty is that Paul could not have envisioned what we, today, think of as a gay or lesbian relationship. His comments clearly addressed some of the darker elements of Roman society, and his goal was to spread Christianity to Gentiles and help them sort out what it meant to be a non-Jewish Christian. It is against this backdrop that we must view his comments about same-sex relations.

Chapter Ten

Jesus and Homosexuality

It always seemed to me a bit pointless to disapprove of homosexuality. It's like disapproving of rain.

—Francis Maude

Silence Speaks Volumes

If you were to only listen to conservative Christian ministers and never actually read the Bible, you would certainly think that Jesus was very anti-gay and that he railed about the evils of homosexuality on a regular basis. You might even get the impression that he made it a central part of his teaching.

From the Pulpit

...What kind of craziness is it in our society which will put a cloak of secrecy around a group of people whose lifestyle is at best abominable. Homosexuality is an abomination. The practices of those people is appalling. It is a pathology. It is a sickness, and instead of thinking of giving these people a preferred status and privacy, we should treat AIDS exactly the same way as any other communicable disease...

—Pat Robertson

[Homosexuals] want to come into churches and disrupt church services and throw blood all around and try to give people AIDS and spit in the face of ministers.

—Pat Robertson

Homosexuality is Satan's diabolical attack upon the family that will not only have a corrupting influence upon our next generation, but it will also bring down the wrath of God upon America.

—Jerry Falwell

Pat Robertson and Jerry Falwell are just two of the more vocal and visible Christian ministers who have made homosexuality a key issue in their quest to preserve "Christian" values. Admittedly, many Christians are not quite so hateful in how they discuss the issue, but the pulpit is often used to drive home the idea that Jesus disapproved of homosexuality, that he believed it to be evil and sinful, and in a few of the more extreme churches, that God actually hates homosexuals.

Given that these ministers claim to speak for Jesus, you would think that they could pelt you with a few quotes from Jesus that clearly denounce homosexuality as an "abomination." Many Christians are surprised to find that this is not the case.

Once, on a bus in San Francisco, I was minding my own business when the man across from me decided that I would be a good target for "saving." He seemed nice enough, so I decided to be polite and hear him out. Once he was done with his initial speech, he invited me to his Bible study group.

I thanked him for inviting me and asked if I could bring my boyfriend. His Christian love quickly turned sour like a glass of milk in the hot sun. "Homosexuality is a sin," he declared.

Underneath it all I'm sure he was a good person, perhaps a better person than I, because I couldn't resist having some fun with him. So I set my trap.

"Says who?" I calmly replied.

"Says Jesus, that's who!" He quickly snapped back.

Bingo! He took the bait. "I'll tell you what. If you can show me all the Bible verses where Jesus denounces homosexuality as a sin, I will come to your Bible study group, and I will even leave my boyfriend at home." He lit up like a shark that had caught the sent of blood. Then I handed him a piece of paper with my email address on it. "If you can't send me Bible passages where Jesus condemns homosexuality, however, I want you to come with me to a service at the Metropolitan Community Church."[44]

He agreed to my little bet and exited the bus at the next stop. I am still waiting for his email.

Most people, Christian and non-Christian alike are shocked to find out that Jesus himself said nothing either for or against homosexuality. And it is this thorny little detail that you will never hear mentioned in a conservative church. Because ministers frequently tell people that Jesus was against homosexuality, their followers assume there is a sound Biblical reason for such a belief.

Adolph Hitler is quoted as saying, "Make the lie big, make it simple, keep saying it, and eventually they will

---

[44] The Metropolitan Community Church (MCC) is a Christian church with a largely queer membership. It was started to give queer people a place to worship at a time when no other Christian denominations were welcoming.

believe it." Just as this principle enabled Hitler to get otherwise good people to do unthinkable acts while others turned their heads as genocide was happening, some of the leaders in the religious right have employed the same technique with horrible consequences for queer people.

Jesus did not utter a single word about homosexual sex, love or relationships. According to the four Gospels and all the known Gnostic Gospels, Jesus never even broached the subject.

In the 2004 presidential election, George W. Bush was very successful in firing up the passions of conservative Christians by using wedge issues such as gay marriage. This strategy helped him win a second term. What is odd is not that a politician would appeal to religious convictions to get votes—politicians have been doing that throughout history. What is odd is that the principles that Jesus taught such as non-violence and helping the poor were not mentioned by Bush. The only issues that seemed to excite conservative Christians were gay rights and abortion—two issues that Jesus never discussed.

If Jesus himself didn't say anything specific about homosexuality one way or the other, all anyone can do is guess what his thoughts on the subject might have been. Conservative Christians have argued that he didn't say anything about it because it was not an issue at that time, but that if Jesus were on earth today, he would certainly denounce gay relationships.

There are several holes in that theory. First, same-sex relationships were all around Jesus. During the time when Jesus was alive, what is now Israel (then Palestine) was controlled by the Roman Empire. Romans, as we noted in the last chapter, were known for their affinity for same-sex relationships. It was not uncommon for a Roman man to have a younger man as a lover, and gay ritual sex and prostitution were common in Roman pagan rituals. It would have been impossible for Jesus not to be aware of this. In fact, in Matthew 8:5-13, Jesus heals a boy who is believed to be the sexual companion of a Roman soldier.[45] In the passage, Jesus does not denounce their relationship, but rather shows compassion to the solider and his young friend by healing the boy.

In light of this, Jesus' silence about this issue speaks volumes. Either Jesus saw nothing wrong with gay relationships, or he didn't feel it was important enough to comment on either way. Certainly it was not a central part of his teaching.

So why such passion on the part of some Christians toward an issue that Jesus didn't think was important enough to mention? No one reading the Bible with an honest and open mind can say that Jesus was *for* or *against* homosexuality as there is no record of him commenting on it. But like many modern issues (e.g., stem cell research) upon which Jesus did not comment, we can look at other matters that Jesus did comment on to get a very good idea of what he would have felt about the issue.

---

[45] Most translations of this passage refer to the young man as a servant or a slave. However, the Greek word used to describe the ailing servant is pais which is the same word used to refer to a same-gender partner. It is also worth noting that not only did Jesus heal the boy, he held the soldier up as an example of what it meant to have true faith. This, of course, is a far cry from how many conservative Christians responded to the AIDS crisis.

Jesus on the Purity Laws

One of the chief arguments that some Christians make for Jesus' silence on homosexuality is that the Old Testament was very clear about it being an abomination, and therefore he didn't need to comment on it. Putting aside the already-noted difficulties with the Purity Laws in Leviticus, there are other good reasons to believe that Jesus would not have given them much stock.

As mentioned in chapter eight, the two major denouncements of homosexuality in the Old Testament are part of the Purity Laws outlined in Leviticus and other books. As noted, most of those laws are seen by even the most conservative of modern Christians as irrelevant. But how did Jesus view those laws? Did he advocate following them?

It is interesting that this very issue caused a huge rift between the Pharisees (Jewish leaders) and Jesus. At the time Jesus was alive, Jews were expected to observe all sorts of laws—ritual washing, circumcision, animal sacrifice, avoiding the "unclean" people, and changing money to non-Roman coins before making an offering. There was so much that people were expected to do in order to be holy that no one could do it all. Jesus denounced the strictness of Jewish leaders in enforcing these laws. "They tie up heavy burdens, hard to bear, and lay them on people's shoulders, but they themselves are not willing to move them with their finger" (Matthew 23:4).

Jesus saw this and recognized that it was nothing more than a system to keep the leaders of the day in power with "long robes" and "[seats] of honor in the

Synagogues" (Luke 20:46), and he willfully and regularly broke these laws to prove his point. At the very heart of Jesus' teaching was the idea that the Purity Laws, originally written to protect people, were outdated and actually holding people back. He saw them as a heavy millstone that people needed to be freed from, so he offered an alternative approach that he described in this way: "My yoke is easy and my burden is light" (Matthew 11:30).

Each time Jesus touched a leper he was breaking the Purity Laws because lepers were believed to be unclean (Leviticus 14). They were outcast and forced to live in leper colonies. When they were out and about, they were required to call out so that people would not accidentally touch them and become themselves unclean.

To touch a leper in Jesus' day was to sentence yourself to the same fate as the lepers—you would be considered unclean and you would certainly not be welcomed in society. Jesus saw this law as outdated and immoral, and he did not just preach against it. He would embrace the lepers and heal them with his touch (Matthew 8:1-4). It is ironic that even today religious leaders will use diseases such as AIDS in much the same way that leprosy was used in Jesus' day.[46]

Likewise, menstruation was also considered very unclean; women on their cycle were not to be touched. It was bad enough for healthy women to be "unclean" for a few days each month, but for a woman described in three of the four Gospels as suffering from a disorder causing her to perpetually bleed,[47] that was a true curse.

---

[46] "AIDS is the wrath of a just God against homosexuals. To oppose it would be like an Israelite jumping in the Red Sea to save one of Pharaoh's charioteers." —Jerry Falwell

[47] Matthew 9:20-22, Mark 5: 26-28, Luke 8: 43-45

This meant an entire life without touch and a life in which people would revile her as unclean. Having heard of Jesus' healing abilities, she decided to go see him.

Not wanting to make him unclean by touching him, she decided to sneak up to him in a large crowd of people and touch his cloak. When she did, she was immediately healed. Jesus became aware that "power" had gone out of him and asked, "Who touched me?" The apostle Peter pointed out that in a crowd of that size, hundreds of people were bumping into him, but Jesus insisted that someone has indeed touched him.

The woman realized she had been caught, so she begged Jesus' forgiveness and explained the situation. According to Jewish law, the proper thing to do would have been to stone this woman. Her touching someone in her unclean state was punishable by death. Jesus had every right to be angry with her; but he was not. He told her "Take heart daughter, your faith has healed you" (Matthew 9:22).

On another occasion a woman was about to be stoned for being caught in adultery (John 8:9). As already mentioned, adultery was an offense punishable by death according to the law (Leviticus 20:10). Jesus, true to form, comes to the woman's aid and tells the crowd that the one free of sin should cast the first stone. No one can do it, and he is left there alone with the woman, to whom he then offers forgiveness.

It wasn't just in the context of healing that Jesus broke the Purity Laws. Once, the Pharisees approached and asked him why his disciples did not follow the laws and wash their hands before they ate. After a heated debate with the Pharisees about the law, Jesus explained to his followers that "what goes into a man's mouth does not make him 'unclean,' but what comes out of his mouth, that is what makes him 'unclean.' ... Don't you see that whatever enters the mouth goes into the stomach and then out of the body? But the things that come out of the mouth come from the heart, and these make a man 'unclean.' For out of the heart come evil thoughts, murder, adultery, sexual immorality, theft, false testimony, slander. These are what make a man 'unclean'; but eating with unwashed hands does not make him 'unclean'" (Matthew 15:19-21).

So what does all this have to do with being queer? A lot. All of the laws that Jesus so willfully broke, from touching the lepers and the bleeding woman to eating without ritually washing his hands first, are laws that come from the same Old Testament books that denounce homosexuality. Jesus clearly felt these laws needed to change and that many of them were no longer useful. Given his willingness to question the Purity Laws, it is very reasonable to assume that he would question the two short passages that mention homosexuality as well.

Jesus and Sodom

OK, so the Purity Laws were outdated and Jesus was one of the first to see this and really take a stand. But what about Sodom? Conservative Christians love to cite the destruction of Sodom as a major reason why homosexuality is sinful. I have already made my case as to why I think this is a misrepresentation of the story—namely, that the true sins of Sodom had nothing to do with gay love, sex or sexual morality, but with not welcoming travelers and showing a lack of hospitality by trying to gang rape the angels who were visiting Lot. Even a coarse reading of the story leaves little room for any other interpretation.

But don't believe me—after all, I'm gay and might have a hidden agenda. To be safe, we should take Jesus at his word once again, this time as he discusses the story of Sodom in the Gospel of Matthew.

To understand Jesus' comments about Sodom, it is important to put them in context. The comments come in a section of Matthew's Gospel called Jesus Sends Out the Twelve (Matthew 10). In this section Jesus gathers his closest followers, the twelve apostles, and instructs them to go out and preach and heal "the lost sheep of Israel."

As he is sending them out into the countryside, he gives them very specific instructions about what to bring, where to stay and how to respond to towns and villages that are not welcoming. In describing towns that are not hospitable toward the apostles, he references Sodom, saying "I tell you the truth, it will be more bearable for Sodom and Gomorrah on the day of judgment than for that town."

As you can see, there is no mention of gay or lesbian sex, no mention of anal intercourse, no mention of gang rape. Clearly Jesus saw the sins of Sodom as being that of inhospitality in general and not welcoming prophets and divine messengers in particular. In much the same way that the city of Sodom was punished for not welcoming God's angels, Jesus is saying that towns that don't welcome the apostles would also be punished.

To take this even further, Jesus had the perfect opportunity to give some moral guidance around homosexuality. He could have said something like, "not only was Sodom not a friendly place, but they were a bunch of perverts too." He did not. And yet, if you listen to any sermon on the subject of homosexuality from a conservative pulpit, they will insist that Jesus was against loving gay relationships and that the Sodom story proves it.

From the Source

These twelve Jesus sent out with the following instructions: "Do not go among the Gentiles or enter any town of the Samaritans. Go rather to the lost sheep of Israel. As you go, preach this message: 'The kingdom of heaven is near.' Heal the sick, raise the dead, cleanse those who have leprosy, drive out demons. Freely you have received, freely give. Do not take along any gold or silver or copper in your belts; take no bag for the journey, or extra tunic, or sandals or a staff; for the worker is worth his keep.

"Whatever town or village you enter, search for some worthy person there and stay at his house until you leave. As you enter the home, give it your greeting. If the home is deserving, let your peace rest on it; if it is not, let your peace return to you. If anyone will not welcome you or listen to your words, shake the dust off your feet when you leave that home or town. I tell you the truth, it will be more bearable for Sodom and Gomorrah on the day of judgment than for that town. I am sending you out like sheep among wolves. Therefore be as shrewd as snakes and as innocent as doves."

Points to Remember

1. Jesus never said anything for or against homosexuality.

2. Living among Romans, Jesus was certainly aware of same-sex relationships.

3. On at least one occasion, Jesus healed a Roman soldier's younger male companion, likely his lover.

4. The very Purity Laws that denounce homosexuality were frequently broken and criticized by Jesus.

5. In the one instance in which Jesus spoke of Sodom, he made no reference to sexuality, gay or straight. Instead, he focused on hospitality.

Chapter Eleven

Love Stories

Everybody's journey is individual. If you fall in love with a boy, you fall in love with a boy. The fact that many Americans consider it a disease says more about them than it does about homosexuality.

—JAMES A. BALDWIN

While there are a number of passages in the Bible that are often used to justify prejudice against queer people, there are some beautiful queer love stories in the Bible as well. You are not likely to hear televangelists talking about these relationships, but they are there, and they do bring comfort to many queer people who have turned to the Bible for guidance.

Ruth and Naomi

If you go to a Christian wedding, you may well hear the following passage read to the bride and groom:

> "Where you go I will go, and where you stay I will stay. Your people will be my people and your God my God. Where you die I will die, and there I will be buried. May the Lord deal with me, be it every so

severely, if anything but death separates you and me."

—Ruth 1:16-17

It is a beautiful passage about love, commitment and family that is poetic and heartfelt. It is easy to see why a couple would want this passage from scripture to punctuate their wedding ceremony. There is a catch, however. This is not a man speaking to a woman, or a woman speaking to a man. It is Ruth speaking to her "close friend," Naomi.

The book of Ruth is very short, and it basically talks about a love affair between two women. Conservative Christians have always maintained that they were not lesbians, but rather two platonic friends who cared very much about one another. True, there is no mention of them "knowing" each other, or "lying down" with one another as one might expect. Let's face it, the Old Testament authors love to talk about sex, and there is no direct mention of Ruth and Naomi being sexually intimate. That, of course, doesn't mean they were not. But at that time, sex had a rigid definition, one that might have gotten Bill Clinton off the hook. Anything that did not involve penetration was not likely viewed as sex.

Aside from the fact that the Old Testament doesn't mention the two women having carnal knowledge of one another, their relationship would make a great lesbian romance novel. The story begins with the death of Naomi's husband Elimelech, leaving Naomi as a widow with two sons—not a very good situation for a woman at that time. One of her sons married Ruth, the other married Orpah. Unfortunately, both of Naomi's sons died as well, leaving Ruth, Naomi and Orpah to fend for them-selves. So Naomi suggests her two daughters-in-law return home and hope to find new husbands.

It is a very emotional scene in which the three women embrace and cry—the makings of a great chick flick, if you will. Ultimately Orpah does decide to return home in the hopes of finding a new husband, but Ruth stays with Naomi, and as they tearfully embrace, Ruth recites the famous passage quoted above that is now a standard at so many weddings.

So in this context, Ruth and Naomi seem like best friends who don't want to part. Although being a single woman in those days was considered a huge curse, trumped only by a woman being unable to bear chil-dren, the two women stayed together. In any event, Ruth's decision to stay with Naomi was a major decision that she had to know would affect the rest of her life.

Where one might think of this as a lesbian love story rather than just a story of two good friends is in how they chose to live with one another. Ruth and Naomi traveled to Bethlehem and arrived just in time for the harvest. Rather than living as two friends, Ruth took on the role of a husband and joined the men in the field harvesting barley. Ultimately Ruth does find a husband and becomes the great-grandmother to King David.

As I said, nothing in this story specifically states that Ruth and Naomi were lovers. However, they did have a very close and highly unusual relationship, which would certainly have raised a few eyebrows. Of course, people tend to think of them in the terms they want to see them in. People who are gay-friendly point to this story as proof that the Bible is not all anti-gay, while conservative Christians take a very different view of the story. In either case, though, the story clearly demonstrates that love and commitment define a family rather than tradition—a theme that queer activists have been speaking to for years.

From the Source

In the days when the judges ruled, there was a famine in the land, and a man from Bethlehem in Judah, together with his wife and two sons, went to live for a while in the country of Moab. The man's name was Elimelech, his wife's name Naomi, and the names of his two sons were Mahlon and Kilion. They were Ephrathites from Bethlehem, Judah. And they went to Moab and lived there.

Now Elimelech, Naomi's husband, died, and she was left with her two sons. They married Moabite women, one named Orpah and the other Ruth. After they had lived there about ten years, both Mahlon and Kilion also died, and Naomi was left without her two sons and her husband.

When she heard in Moab that the LORD had come to the aid of his people by providing food for them, Naomi and her daughters-in-law prepared to return home from there. With her two daughters-in-law she left the place where she had been living and set out on the road that would take them back to the land of Judah.

Then Naomi said to her two daughters-in-law, "Go back, each of you, to your mother's home. May the LORD show kindness to you, as you have shown to your dead and to me. May the LORD grant that each of you will find rest in the home of another husband." Then she kissed them and they wept aloud and said to her, "We will go back with you to your people."

But Naomi said, "Return home, my daughters. Why would you come with me? Am I going to have any more sons, who could become your husbands? Return home, my daughters; I am too old to have another husband. Even if I thought there was still hope for me—even if I had a husband tonight and then gave birth to sons—would you wait until they grew up? Would you remain unmarried for them? No, my daughters. It is more bitter for me than for you, because the LORD's hand has gone out against me!"

At this they wept again. Then Orpah kissed her mother-in-law good-by, but Ruth clung to her.

"Look," said Naomi, "your sister-in-law is going back to her people and her gods. Go back with her."

But Ruth replied, "Don't urge me to leave you or to turn back from you. Where you go I will go, and where you stay I will stay. Your people will be my people and your God my God. Where you die I will die, and there I will be buried. May the LORD deal with me, be it ever so severely, if anything but death separates you and me." When Naomi realized that Ruth was determined to go with her, she stopped urging her.

So the two women went on until they came to Bethlehem. When they arrived in Bethlehem, the whole town was stirred because of them, and the women exclaimed, "Can this be Naomi?"

"Don't call me Naomi, " she told them. "Call me Mara, because the Almighty has made my life very bitter. I went away full, but the LORD has brought me back empty. Why call me Naomi? The LORD has afflicted me; the Almighty has brought misfortune upon me."

So Naomi returned from Moab accompanied by Ruth the Moabitess, her daughter-in-law, arriving in Bethlehem as the barley harvest was beginning.

—Ruth 1:1-22

Jonathan and David

The books Samuel I and II describe a very tender and loving relationship between King David, a central figure in the Old Testament, and Jonathan, the son of King Saul. Unlike Ruth and Naomi, David and Jonathan's relationship was a bit more defined.

The story goes something like this: Jonathan was the rightful heir to King Saul's throne, but for reasons not worth noting here, Saul wants David to become king. However, when David meets Saul's son Jonathan, they experience an instant connection that is described in this way: "Jonathan became one in spirit with David and he loved him as himself."

David then moves in with Jonathan's family to be with him. The Bible also gives a fairly strong indication that they were sexually intimate, saying "And Jonathan made a covenant with David because he loved him as himself. Jonathan took off the robe he was wearing and gave it to David, along with his tunic and even his sword and belt."

So, to put it another way, rather than finding a wife, David moved in with Jonathan and his family, and Jonathan then professed his love for David and took off all his clothes. It's kind of hard to spin that one, but conservative Christians will maintain they were just good friends. I wonder what Pat Robertson would say if Ted Haggard said to him "I love you" and took off his clothes. My guess is he would not view that as just a friendly overture.

Saul was interested in David as well and wanted nothing more than to have him be part of the family, so he tried to fix him up with his daughter Merab, who rejected him. Then Saul tried to fix him up with his other daughter Michal. The Bible doesn't really say too much about this marriage, but the impression given is that it is to get David in the family so he can become king.

So, back to Jonathan and David's relationship. Their connection grew, and on two different occasions the Bible mentions them being very close. 1 Samuel 20:40 says, "...David got up from the south side of the stone and bowed down before Jonathan three times, with his face to the ground. Then they kissed each other and wept together, but *David wept the most*."[48]

In the first chapter of the second book of Samuel, David finds out that both Jonathan and his father Saul have been killed. Filled with grief, David says, "I grieve for you Jonathan, my brother. You were very dear to me. Your love for me was wonderful, more wonderful than that of a woman." This of course is an odd thing to say, especially since men and women at that time were not social—you were either married to a woman or she was your sister or mother. David's referral to a woman's love certainly implied a romantic relationship.

---

[48] The phrase "David wept the most" is sometimes translated as "David became great," which some have speculated implies that David got an erection. I think that is a bit of a reach, but kissing each other and crying together seems pretty gay with or without "becoming great."

The stories of Jonathan and David and Ruth and Naomi are a bit hazy if for no other reason than the Bible writers loved to tiptoe around the edges when it came to sex, and certainly had an affinity for double entendres.

What is important is that some of the central figures in the Old Testament would likely identify as gay or lesbian if they were alive today. They expressed great love and that love carried them through. It is unfortunate that conservative Christianity ignores these love stories while twisting other Bible stories to fit their own preconceptions about homosexuality.

I believe that gay, lesbian and transgendered people can look to these stories for strength and courage, and those who support us can take comfort in these love stories because they affirm the value, worth and importance of queer people throughout history.

Conclusion

On October 6, 1998, a young man named Matthew Shepard was beaten, tied to a fence on a rural road outside of Laramie, Wyoming and left to die. He was brought to a hospital in Fort Collins, Colorado where he died six days later, his family by his side.

You have probably heard this story because it garnered such media attention. This tragedy created a shift in which things began to change. The gruesome details of this crime were so shocking that much of straight America was forced to look at violence against queer people for the first time. Matthew Shepard was not the first person to die because of sexual orientation, and, sadly, he won't be the last.

At his funeral, a group of "Christians" from the Westborough Baptist Church, led by The Reverend Fred Phelps, decided to stage a protest. Phelps and his followers were well known in the queer community, as they would frequently show up at prominent gay funerals to taunt the grieving with signs bearing such awful slogans as "God Hates Fags" and "Fags Die, God Laughs".

Several years before, I had started *Daily Wisdom,* an email list to which I would send out a daily inspirational quote. A woman named Jane Harper emailed me and asked me to use this list to help raise funds for her Bigot-O-Thon. She had heard that Phelps was planning to protest Matthew's funeral and she wanted to do something to counter his hatred. Her plan was both simple and beautiful. She asked me to forward the following note to my list:

> Rev. Fred Phelps and his cohorts plan to crash the funeral with their "No Tears for Queers" protest. I spoke to Tammy Pace of the First National Bank in Fort Collins, Colorado. They are handling the Matthew Shepard Memorial Fund. The idea of a Bigot-O-Thon was appealing to her. I also spoke with the Casper, Wyoming police department about tomorrow's protest and getting an accurate bigot-count. The idea is this: For every bigot Rev. Fred Phelps flies in from Kansas, or who joins his protest locally, we will pledge donations (like a Walk-A-Thon) per head (penny, nickel, dime, quarter, dollar, etc) depending on our income level, and mail a check for that amount to *The Matthew Shepard Memorial Fund.*
>
> Please mark: "For Bigot-O-Thon" in the memo part of the check. Tammy Pace said she will pass this news on to Matthew's family when she speaks with them later. I will contact several of the news agencies shortly. The funeral is less than 24 hours away, we need to move fast. We can make a positive statement with relatively little effort. Pass the word, pass the hat at work... whatever. C'mon... we can do this and stick a lemon to the Rev. Fred Phelps!
>
> —Jane Harper

The beauty of this plan was that the more "successful" Phelps was in whipping up hatred, the more money would be raised. Jane informed me afterward that she sent Reverend Phelps a thank you note for helping to raise so much money.

Shortly after Matthew's funeral, Phelps flew to San

Francisco for another round of protests. This time, his target was the local gay-friendly Christian churches. It didn't take long for church leaders to figure out what was going on and a call was put out to notify other congregations that Phelps was in town and making his rounds.

When he showed up at the local Metropolitan Community Church, its predominately queer congregation was ready. One might expect that, after all Phelps had done to kick our community during the times of the greatest grief, this congregation would come out with pitchforks to run him out of town. But they had something much more effective in mind. When Phelps showed up with his protesters and hateful signs, the congregation came out of the church and began to sing, "This little light of mine, I'm going to let it shine." The protesters eventually left in frustration.

It is important to note that even the most conservative Christian leaders have denounced the actions of Fred Phelps. He in no way represents conservative Christianity as a whole. But it is also important to note that many ministers who are embarrassed by Phelps' over-the-top hatred are the same ones who have no problem misrepresenting the story of Sodom, or taking the Purity Laws out of context. They have no issue with allowing people to believe that Jesus condemned homosexuality when he didn't.

The reason so many conservatives dislike Phelps is that he presents a public relations nightmare for them in the way he so hatefully expresses himself. I have often said that he has done more to garner support for queer people than just about anyone else. And his assertion that "God Hates Fags" is just a particularly disgusting way of saying God thinks homosexuals are an "abomination."

Whether they are blaming the 9/11 attacks[49] on gays or sending gay teens to "rehabilitation" centers to "heal" them of their homosexuality, the message is not that much different from the underlying philosophy that guides Phelps. They simply sugar coat the poison pill by saying "love the sinner, hate the sin." Standing at the pulpit and telling the world that God thinks homosexuals are an abomination creates a justification for the way gays, lesbians and transgender people are treated in our society. And while that doesn't always lead to murder, it does often lead to many other forms of abuse and mistreatment.

Thankfully, most of us will never experience the horror of being beaten and left to die the way Matthew Shepard did. Most of our families will not have to endure the grief that Judy and Roger Shepard will endure for the rest of their lives. But to a lesser degree, all queer people feel the sting of oppression and nothing is more painful for a parent, brother, sister, son or daughter than to hear that their family member was attacked. Most of these attacks are justified by conservative churches. Until we address "Christian"-inspired hate speech about homo-

---

51 "...throwing God out of the public square, out of the schools, the abortionists have got to bear some burden for this because God will not be mocked and when we destroy 40 million little innocent babies, we make God mad...I really believe that the pagans and the abortionists and the feminists and the gays and the lesbians who are actively trying to make that an alternative lifestyle, the ACLU, People for the American Way, all of them who try to secularize America...I point the thing in their face and say you helped [9/11] happen."
—Jerry Fallwell, The 700 Club, September 13, 2001

sexuals, we will never make lasting progress in the quest for equality for all people.

Shortly after Matthew Shepard died, I saw a prominent conservative minister on TV talking about the Christian response to this tragedy. He was quick to denounce the violence, which was certainly a step in the right direction. But then he said something very telling. As if he deserved a Boy Scout merit badge for it, he boasted that his congregation had prayed for Matthew Shepard's soul. They prayed that Matthew had found Jesus in his last suffering hours on that fence and that he had renounced his homosexual lifestyle so that he would be able to go to heaven. There was no talk of praying for the young men who had murdered Matthew, no concern for their souls, no hoping that in their jail cells they would find Jesus. They were murderers and thugs and yet, in his opinion, it was Matthew's soul that needed saving.

Meanwhile, Judy and Roger Shepard showed mercy and in a statement to the court asked that Matthew's murderers be allowed to live. No one would have blamed them for seeking the death penalty—in fact there were many who would have applauded them. But they courageously chose to respond to the violence against their son with compassion and mercy.

As you go about your life and encounter Christians who believe homosexuality to be a sin and who want to deny homosexuals their basic human rights, know that you can make a difference. You can't change every mind and you can't open every heart, but you can change some. Just as sermons against interracial marriage or in favor of racial segregation are no longer accepted, there will come a time once enough hearts and minds have been changed when conservative Christians will look back on their current doctrines regarding homosexuals as a very dark chapter in their history. Until then, we need all the help we can get to respectfully take a stand.

In much the same way that the chanting of "This Little Light of Mine" frustrated the anti-gay protesters instead of joining them in their rage, letting our own light shine is the only way we can address this affront to human dignity. In much the same way that Matthew's parents chose not to respond to violence with more violence, we must, to a much lesser degree, learn to do the same.

We don't need to be pushy, preachy or obnoxious. We don't need to raise our voices or resort to name-calling. We don't need to criticize or denigrate a person's faith. We simply need to speak truth and stand tall. As I have tried to demonstrate in this book, we have the facts on our side. Now all that is needed is for each of us to do our part in changing *Hearts and Minds*.

Part Three
Essays

Touched by Religious Intolerance

Homosexuality is assuredly no advantage, but it is nothing to be ashamed of, no vice, no degradation, it cannot be classified as an illness; we consider it to be a variation of the sexual function produced by a certain arrest of sexual development. Many highly respectable individuals of ancient and modern times have been homosexuals, several of the greatest men among them (Plato, Michelangelo, Leonardo da Vinci, etc.). It is a great injustice to persecute homosexuality as a crime, and cruelty too...

If [your son] is unhappy, neurotic, torn by conflicts, inhibited in his social life, analysis may bring him harmony, peace of mind, full efficiency whether he remains a homosexual or gets changed...

—SIGMUND FREUD[52]

In the early church, it was customary for Christians to stand up and share their experience. If they had fallen short and sinned or if they had experienced a miracle or revelation, they would share that with their community. In Twelve Step programs they refer to this process as sharing "Experience, Strength and Hope."

Living in San Francisco, I am blessed to be surrounded by healthy queer people with whom I can share my story and from whom I hear stories that help me grow and heal as well. Not all people are so lucky. Perhaps you live in an area where there are few other queer people or where you feel like you are alone in supporting your son, daughter, brother or sister.

I have invited a number of people with inspiring stories to share their experiences, strength and hope here. While no two people will have the exact same story, know that there are others out there who have struggled with religious intolerance and not only come out on the other side, but flourished, and can help us along our own journey.

—Darren

[50] Reprinted in Jones, 1957, pp. 208-209, from *The American Journal of Psychiatry,* 1951, 107, 786

The Dream of a New Language

by Laura C. Engelken

It is perhaps not a perfect analogy, but I liken it to being bilingual—the ability to speak the Christian dialects of conservative and progressive. I acquired these two different languages for understanding and communicating about the divine through my personal experiences and various faith communities—both out of choice and necessity.

In high school, I chose to accept Jesus as savior—becoming "born again" in response to God's unconditional love. As a teenager struggling for self-worth and meaning, connecting with a love that embraced me despite all my faults and self-doubts was a necessity. However, when coming out to myself and others as a lesbian in my early twenties, God's great love became conditional upon my sexuality. My spiritual and physical survival then became dependent upon finding a new language—one that assigned me worth and dignity as a child of God—worth and dignity that came with my sexuality and not in spite of it. This choice to describe the boundless love and nature of God using a new and different vocabulary from my fundamentalist past was a necessity.

Theologian Elizabeth Johnson emphasizes that our symbols for God shape our experience and construct our world. For example, if we only envision God as male—calling him "Father"—we readily embrace patriarchal power structures as the only appropriate way to "do church." This deification of a particular gender translates to sexuality as well and thus heterosexual partnerships become the only acceptable expression of God's divine gift of sexual love. Consequently, I resonate more with names and descriptions such as Holy One and the Divine rather than Father or King. Even the language of "God" does not particularly work for me, given the default assumption of divine masculinity—an unquestioned association similar to assumed heterosexuality.

Yet, when talking with friends and acquaintances whose language reflects a more conservative Christian theology and perspective of the world, I often choose words and concepts familiar to their ears although they taste somewhat foreign on my tongue. Too often we demonize people who speak a different language—particularly regarding the holy—and thus derail opportunities for understanding and connection before conversation occurs. At times it is a tongue-twisting challenge to honor and express the realities of who I am and what I believe in a way that can be conceptualized and understood by a conservative Christian, yet which creates space for new understandings and possibilities for all of us.

This engagement with a language and worldview that does not fully resonate with the core of who you are—and may even render pieces of you invisible—takes significant energy. It is a cultural immersion that makes it even more important to find communities that speak your own language. It is crucial to find faith communities and friends with whom you can let your tongue wag freely and draw upon shared meanings and vocabulary as you develop relationships with each other, yourself and the divine.

When you are an exchange student, there comes a time when you begin dreaming in your new language. I have begun dreaming in mine—dreaming of a life fully affirmed by the divine, dreaming of a faith community where I can be loved and love in return and not considered a project or a liability, and dreaming of attending seminary to pursue ordination within the United Church of Christ. All these dreams have become reality, as I have learned with joy and humility that no language can fully capture the great and wondrous nature of the divine.

Laura C. Engelken (left) is a Seminary student at Pacific School of Religion in Berkeley, CA. She welcomes your emails at lauraengelken@darrenmain.com

Just A Little Patience

by Jasper Trout

When I finally came out to both my mother and father, after at least six years of being "out" to myself, their response wasn't really what I had hoped for. My mom just looked at me with watery eyes while my dad on the other hand proceeded to tell me that this was simply impossible because "being gay" didn't exist.

I guess you have to know a little of my family history to understand what a huge and personally stressful event telling my parents about my sexual orientation was.

Growing up in my house meant going to church three times a week, prayer before every meal, family bible study and gold stars for proselytizing my schoolmates. It also meant that certain subjects were taboo. The ideas of any non-Christian religions, interracial families or sex—sexuality, sexual orientation, even procreation (beyond that crew of storks that dropped neatly wrapped babies on the doorstep)—were all taboo. We just didn't talk about them. They made my father completely uncomfortable and when he was uncomfortable everyone in the house was uncomfortable.

I remember exactly one discussion relating to sex between my father and me. Actually, to call it a discussion is a stretch, it was more of a brief and dire warning and left me with more confusion than clarity.

One evening, just before dinner, he called me to "have a talk." As always, this consisted of retiring to somewhere in the house where no one else was so that his words would not be interrupted. We walked down the long hall to my bedroom at the back of the house. He turned around and looked down at me, his face showed such obvious discomfort that I immediately internalized feeling very awkward myself.

"I've got to tell you something," he began. "There are BAD people out in the world. They're called gay... or queers. They have parades. They might try to get you to do bad things. Steer clear of these people... OK, let's go eat dinner."

Wow, my twelve-year-old mind thought. I think I just got my "Birds and the Bees" talk. What does that mean?

Years later, when my own feelings of attraction toward other boys began to emerge, this "talk" loomed in my head. This, and the one other time that homosexuality had come up in our family—when my father expressed to my mother feeling "sick to his stomach" after speaking on the phone with a receptionist at a Guerneville motel who sounded, in his words, like "that, that funny fellow on *Hello, Sydney*"; he didn't mean "ha, ha, funny" (*Hello Sydney* was a TV show in the late 70's or early 80's starring the clean guy from *The Odd Couple* where he played an openly gay character—perhaps the first ever on network TV?)

Growing up in a Christian household, with parents whose social network consisted almost exclusively of other members of the church and in a society where the most stinging schoolyard taunt was to be called a "fag", it took me many years to finally be able to accept within myself that I was attracted to others of my sex and that could be OK. To actually say that out loud to my peers much less to my parents was, for years, unthinkable.

So finally, six years after beginning the process of accepting in my own heart that I am gay, I set about to close a very important circle and let two of the most important people in my life know my truth.

As I said, their reaction was not exactly what I had hoped for. My father was in complete denial and my mother just looked sad. I'm not sure what I was expecting, but in some fragile little naive place I think I had hoped that they would say something like, "Well, we aren't really happy to know that but you're our son and we love you no matter what. If you're happy, we're happy for you."

Now that's funny—and this time I do mean "ha ha funny."

My father, not one to articulate his ideas in particularly thoughtful or eloquent speech, simply choose to remain in total denial. He even refused to read the letter I had written to them as a "back-up" in case I completely wimped out and didn't tell them at the lunch date I had set up for the purpose. My mother on the other hand has always been my ally and it's to her, I believe, that I owe my ability to both listen and to express myself in a thoughtful way. Over the course of the next few years she wrote me more than one lengthy and articulate letter outlining her beliefs relating to homosexuality, her biblical faith, her fears for my physical and spiritual health and ultimately her unequivocal and unconditional love for me and for my son, her grandson. Yet despite these communications we remained unable to really build a full relationship. I found myself editing everything I said when I would visit or speak on the telephone. Our communications became fewer and fewer as I found that I was afraid to tell them anything about my life in the fear that they would be uncomfortable—or worse—judgmental toward me.

This continued for years, with me annually making the classic holiday pilgrimages to their home for holiday dinners and gatherings. I would bring my son but leave my partner to fend for himself, knowing that he would not be welcome and not wanting to put anyone in an uncomfortable position.

Finally, last year, I realized that the man I have chosen to spend my life with could not be ostracized—however subtly—in this ridiculous dance of denial. I couldn't talk about him at Christmas dinner, couldn't mention any of the vacations or activities we participated in, really didn't have much to talk about with my blood family because so much of my life involves my partner. I had had enough of this dishonest perpetuation of unreality. So I made a decision. This year, we would have the Thanksgiving dinner gathering at our house. I proceeded to invite my sisters and my parents. After getting no response from my parents and with the day quickly approaching I stopped in to invite them again.

Our conversation quickly devolved into them telling me that they would not "validate" my lifestyle by coming into my house and sharing a meal with me and my partner. I was hurt. I was angry. I shouted that that was fine, if that was how they felt then neither I nor my son would ever again set foot in their house. Then I stormed out, slamming the door behind me.

For almost a year we rarely saw each other. With the exception of the occasional game or school play that one of the kids was in and that we all attended we didn't talk or see each other. It hurt me. I can only imagine how much it pained my parents.

But during this most recent holiday season something changed. It has felt like the warm aroma of a spring afternoon, coming on the heels of a cold, hopeless frozen winter. Out of the blue, a week or so before Thanksgiving I got a call from my mother.

"Your dad and I would like to invite you all to our house for Thanksgiving dinner this year," she said.

"You mean all of us, Donny too?" I asked.

She assured me yes, all of us. She was quick to let me know that their views on homosexuality had not changed but that they would rather have us all be a part of each others lives rather than continue this limbo of living not more than five miles apart yet rarely having any contact.

I thanked her, hung up and just smiled. I didn't know how much it would mean to me to have them open just that little crack of tolerance but it was immense.

We've had three or four family gatherings now that we've all attended and the vibe has been nothing but positive.

I think that the lesson I've taken from these experiences is that speaking my truth is most important and sticking to it is vital. But the most telling lesson I've learned is that patience is not only a virtue but essential. Allowing my parents the time they needed to process the implications of intolerance and the space to find their own voice in opening the door to communion led us all to the place we are now. We are creating a positive family relationship and all enjoying the unique and beautiful gifts each of us has to offer. I know that my parents do love me and I hope they know that I love them very much too.

Jasper Trout (right) is a graphic designer and renowned photographer from Napa, California. You can contact Jasper through his website www.troutfarmphotodesign.com or by email at jaspertrout@darrenmain.com

God and Gays:
Bridging the Gap

by Luane Beck and Kim Clark

My story is interesting when juxtaposed with my partner Kim's story.

When I was born, I was immediately baptized Lutheran. Before I was old enough to remember, my parents began going to a Baptist church where we stayed for the majority of my childhood. I loved that church and the people who attended. I went to most of the study groups, my best friend was the Pastor's daughter, and my first kiss was with the Pastor's son. This was my life... until we moved.

After a few months in our new city, we met the Mormon family across the street. Before long, we were attending the Mormon church. As with the Baptist church, my family got very involved. My parents taught classes and chaperoned events. The difference was that I didn't feel comfortable and couldn't relate to my new friends. The primary reason for this discomfort was the belief that "if you weren't Mormon, you wouldn't be saved." That meant all these people I grew up with, all my friends that I loved were going to hell. I couldn't agree with this. Thinking this belief was unique to the Mormon church, I fought long and hard with my mom to let me stop attending that church.

Once in high school, I made some friends that attended the Church of Christ and I started going to church with them… and I do mean started. I went to just a few functions before I learned that the Bible is absolutely not open to interpretation, so what I learned in the past from the other two churches I had attended was absolutely incorrect. I said, "Well, these other churches think they're right, so how do you know you're not wrong?" I was told the Church of Christ is the only "true" church and, you got it, if you weren't fortunate enough to attend there, you were not going to be saved. That meant that now the Mormons and the Baptists were going to hell. Didn't matter if you dedicated your entire life to God, if you didn't dedicate it in the Church of Christ you were going to hell.

This was a blessing. I stopped going to church altogether, but missed the relationship with God and began to build that on my own. This is really the key. I read somewhere that Carl Jung said the main function of formalized religion is to protect people against a direct experience of God. When you really allow yourself to experience God, miracles will begin to happen in your life. Since I had been working on surrendering to God for a few years before I came out, coming out was actually a very easy, awakening experience. I felt like He was holding my hand step by step. I was exceptionally aware that I was falling in love with a soul, not a body. That's not to say I didn't run into some resistance from people. I lost some friends and had a really hard time with my mom, but when you're surrendering to God, He'll get you through. You just have to trust Him.

What I've learned since is that anything based in fear

is not of God. If what you're saying, feeling, thinking is of love, then it's of God.

Now, I believe everywhere is my church. When I get a cup of coffee or I'm at the grocery store, everywhere, I need to remember who God is and how He wants me to treat people. I remember He is always with me even when things don't seem to be going my way. Mostly, I strive to live in a constant state of gratitude for all that He has brought me—including the beautiful trees lining the mountains outside our window.

My partner, Kim, had the opposite experience. She was raised Christian. She went to the same denomination all of her life and didn't know that there were options out there. Her whole life was her church; all of her friends were at that church and not only was her boyfriend of nine years at that church, his stepfather was the Pastor. She was on her way to building the perfect Christian life.

…Until her new roommate moved in. Apparently, she had a very cute behind… I say this with a hint of irony since a common misperception is that gay people are attracted to each other solely for sex, which is the furthest thing from the truth. We crave the same closeness as opposite sex couples and find that intimacy with a member of the same sex.

Kim fought her attraction for months before the two began talking about exploring the feelings they were having for one another. Once they were finally together, Kim and her roommate had a very tempestuous relationship while Kim tried desperately to reconcile her feelings. She told her boyfriend, whom she was in pre-engagement counseling with, that she had feelings for a woman, but never really "left" him. This did not go over well with her roommate, but Kim couldn't bring herself to own her sexuality. She began to numb herself out so much that for a time she contemplated suicide. She believed that people would be relieved of a burden if she were gone. Ultimately, Kim could not commit herself to her roommate. The roommate left and asked to never be contacted again. This took Kim years to get over.

She resumed her relationship with her boyfriend and went on happily for another couple of years. Of course, we can never run from who we are, and she met another woman. This time she did break up with her boyfriend, but still had a really hard time accepting who God made her to be. Fortunately, she went into therapy. Things were tough; although she was committing to her new girlfriend, she was mourning their relationship. Love came with the high price of being judged by the world. She lost all of her friends and had to find another church to attend.

Through prayer, therapy, and a poster that said "God don't make no junk," Kim finally was able to begin to slowly accept who she is.

When I heard her story, I couldn't believe the pain and suffering caused by religion. I'm living proof it does not have to be that way.

When I met Kim she was still very closeted; only a select few were allowed to know that she had a girlfriend. We met at work and, definitely, nobody at work was allowed to know. However, I couldn't let go of her story; I still don't understand using God as a way to condemn people. That is so far from what God wants that I had to make a documentary about it. Now, Kim has not only come out at work, but has also come out to the world. We now attend an omnifaith church where everyone is accepted and all religions worship together. There, we focus on the oneness of all religions and everyone.

The biggest impact the conservative view of homosexuality has had on our life is the negation of rights that we would have if we weren't gay. The FMA was the catalyst for my starting the documentary. We all have to speak out, be out, and let everyone know we are not the "lifestyle" they demonize us to be!

Our advice: Get to God!

Luane Beck is the director and screenwriter of the groundbreaking documentary God and Gays: Bridging the Gap *and Kim Clark, her partner, is the film's producer. They live in the San Francisco Bay Area. You can contact them and learn more about the film at www.godandgaysthemovie.com*

Religious and Spiritual Healing

by James Guay

It's no wonder I grew up to become a psychotherapist offering guidance to other lesbian, gay, bisexual, transgender, queer and questioning (LGBTQQ) individuals to help them heal from religious homophobia and abuse. I grew up the son of a well-known pastor in a relatively insular environment in San Fernando Valley, California. I remember reading the Bible several times through with my family from a very early age. Our religious beliefs were integrated into everything we did as a family. We were in a fundamentalist non-denominational Christian church of well over 10,000 members. My father had made his way through the ranks to become second in command.

By twelve years old, I had known for a few years that I had same-sex attractions but did not yet equate that to the word "homosexuality" I so rarely heard at church. When I finally heard it at church, those around me used it with great disgust. I prayed for hours on end, constantly read the Bible, went to whatever sermon I could, and was fervent in my devotion toward God. While I appeared as the "ultimate" Christian, I was desperate to liberate myself from being gay. I felt as though God had rejected my prayers. How could a merciful and loving God not listen to someone who truly wanted to be saved? Why had God abandoned me?

One day, out of sheer fear of going to hell, I went into the local Christian bookstore and came across the only book on homosexuality I could find. How could I avoid being despised by others I loved? What measures could I take to control my desires? With trembling hands, I went up to the cash register clerk to purchase my newfound hope for change. Despite being a very insecure and shy child, my conviction to rid myself of these desires was so intense that I was determined to find the remedy! It didn't take courage to do this; my heart was fueled by fear and self-hatred.

I read the book from cover to cover realizing only six years and many books later that no substantive change would occur. When I was even more hopeless and distraught as a teenager, I told my dad about my attraction to men and asked for his help. He quickly found me an "ex-gay Christian Psychologist" who tried to guide me into heterosexuality. I also went to ex-gay Christian conferences as the youngest participant and went through a 20-week re-programming workshop, all to no avail. While it took off some of the shame I had felt in recognizing I wasn't the only one out there "struggling" with this, it didn't change my inner-felt sense of who I was and am: a gay man.

I began to research other ways of interpreting the Bible, and multiple ways of leading a healthy gay "lifestyle." Could I really be damned for eternal life because of my love for another man? Why would God not help me change my relational and sexual desires? I discovered it took the same amount of faith to believe in the goodness of me being gay as what I was taught to believe from childhood. I surrounded myself with people who would accept all of who I was instead of preaching "I love you but hate your sin." I realized those comments were impossible. You can't love a sweater without loving the yarn. You can't love the ocean without loving the water. Being gay is too interwoven into who I am as God created me.

I've thoroughly enjoyed becoming a psychotherapist and learning more about how we operate at our best. I've been fortunate enough to assist other LGBTQQ people go through their self-discovery in becoming more fully what God intended them to be. Being there for clients who share their life stories of spiritual trauma when they've been assaulted, harassed, rejected and kicked out of homes, simply for being them, has been deeply moving. I assist clients in healing and growing from these experiences in such a way that they can thrive in the present moment.

Seventeen years after my own parents kicked me out of their home for being gay, healing is still taking place. I'm proud to say that another event helped bridge the gap between my parents and me. Last month my parents apologized for kicking me out of their home and the way that it all happened. While I never thought I would hear these words come from them, and many people don't ever hear such things, perseverance and steadfastness created a window of opportunity for this to occur. Speaking my truth with love, and at times with strong boundaries, paved the way. I enjoy encouraging others to honor themselves and have healthier relationships with others.

Religious homophobia often results in prejudice, negative stereotyping and discrimination against LGBTQQ individuals. It is a form of oppression used by some religious people and institutions to motivate people to change their sexual orientation or sexual behavior. In its most extreme form, religious homophobia can contribute to increased suicide rates, depression, anxiety, difficulties with intimacy, self-hatred, polarization of families and communities, and motivation to try and change one's sexual orientation. Therapy can help you to heal from these experiences and realign with the beauty of who you are at your core, whatever this happens to be.

The process of healing and growth can be different for different people. For some, religious homophobia can be experienced as abusive or even traumatic. They may find strength in recognizing this and processing it similar to how others have healed through other kinds of trauma. For others, understanding their spiritual beliefs anew can be more of a focus of attention. Whatever the need, there are supportive people and groups to help you along the way. It's important to remember that while we are sometimes hurt and injured in relationships, we are also healed in the context of relationships.

James Guay is a Licensed Marriage & Family Therapist (MFC #39252) in San Francisco, California. He specializes in recovery from religious abuse. You can contact him through his office at 415-317-0639 or through his website, www.jamestherapy.com

Leaving the Church and Finding Love

by Kathy Ascare

When I was a young woman, I prayed very hard to become a mother. My prayers were answered with three beautiful children. The years of child raising were both rewarding and challenging. Through the challenges of my life, the Catholic Church was the one stable thing and I looked there for emotional support. While I did find some support, I also felt that I would never be good enough and the guilt trips were constant. As the years passed, new challenges presented themselves and the church didn't always offer useful support. Many times the advice they gave did little more than increase my guilt and shame.

When my oldest son Darren announced he was gay, it was huge for me because the church taught that being gay was a sin. I wanted everyone to love Darren and dreaded the thought of telling my friends about his being gay. Now that I have ignored the church and accepted Darren I have grown in many ways. I have now met many of Darren's gay friends—I love them all!

Attending church is no longer an option. Ten years ago I remarried and was not accepted in my parish in much the same way they rejected my son. They told me going to church was fine, as was contributing money each week, but my husband and I were not allowed to receive the Eucharist. Around this time the church was saying things like "Please find it in your heart to forgive" all the accused priests who violated our children and the Bishops who graciously moved these disturbed men from parish to parish without feeling any remorse! I read somewhere that 60% of the priests are gay. Odd that the Catholic Church teaches that being homosexual is a sin. Why am I confused?

I used to feel bitter but today I am very happy. My faith is strong. I now believe that God is available to us everywhere, not just behind the walls of churches. I have made many mistakes in life but have learned valuable lessons from each. I know in my heart that Darren, and all gay people, were created by a loving God and they are perfect in His eyes. Darren is one of my finest gifts and I would be very sad if he couldn't express his true being. Everyone deserves to be happy whether heterosexual, bisexual, homosexual or whatever. I believe that we must be careful when expressing ourselves not to offend our brothers and sisters the way so many Christian churches have done.

I end with this: I love you Darren and I will go to my grave knowing God loves you too! Love, Mom

Kathy Ascare lives in Pawcatuck, CT with her husband Don. She is the mother of three children (I'm lucky to be one of them) and former member of the Roman Catholic Church. She is currently a pastry chef. She welcomes your emails at kathyascare@darrenmain.com.

Reconciled

by Jason Warner

The Bible says "Ask and you shall receive." We receive not, because we ask not. I don't expect you to change your beliefs because of what I, or anyone else, says or believes. Your belief system and your own spiritual journey are exactly that—yours. I will share my beliefs, and try to explain why I believe what I believe, and I hope you will consider my truth. If nothing else, I simply ask you to respect it.

I will try to cover some of my own experience of reconciling my sexuality with my spirituality. This requires a lot of thought, time, and depth. You can't tell someone how you've reconciled your sexuality with your faith in a few simple words. I wish you could! It would make life so much easier!

See, I understand where those in opposition to homosexuality come from, because I was once one of those people. I believed that the "Word" of God said something very clearly and I tried to live my life accordingly. I was raised in the Pentecostal church. I also traveled with "Truth," a band in the contemporary Christian music industry, and then with another Christian band that was about to be signed by a record label. Before being signed, I felt led to "come out" to the group and tell them about this struggle I had kept secret for 22 years because I felt I couldn't do it alone any longer and I needed "help."

By this time, I knew I was gay and that this was my sexual orientation. I had been to every prayer circle, been anointed with oil, had hands laid on me, prayed for, prayed with, begged and pleaded God to "change me." I even tried exorcism. I love God more than life itself, and I had always known God had a call for me in ministry, through song in particular. I was expected to be the next Steven Curtis Chapman. But, I remained *me*, and thank God I did, because now I love who I am and it's the very person I am that has allowed me to learn what I have learned, search what I have searched, and become the man of God I have become.

It's easy to believe what you believe when it's what you've been taught and told your entire life. But, when you have to actually *search*, and find your own belief system, based on your own truth and experience, it's an entirely new ball game. You have to actually do your homework, and listen to that *still small voice*, and not simply blindly follow someone else's truth. This is why we are here—to learn—and we learn through experience, and we experience through lessons, and we always come back to God giving thanks for those lessons learned.

Unfortunately, the group kicked me out (actually kicked me off the bus after I told them), because they had no idea how to handle the situation. These guys were my brothers and yet they didn't want to hear my heart, my struggle, my pain, my questions, my longing to have someone simply understand and tell me I was going to be OK. They chose to judge, condemn, and throw stones. Hmmm... sound familiar? They reacted this way mostly out of fear. I quickly realized that I had to do something to help others who had gone through similar circumstances or who would face this same situation. I was saddened to realize that the people and communities with whom we should feel the safest in coming out—our friends, families, loved ones, and in particular our churches—are sometimes the people or places we fear the most.

Leaving the band was the best thing that happened to me, because it forced me to start searching for who God was and is to me, and for my calling in life. This search has opened amazing doors and God has been blessing me on the road in full-time ministry now for ten years since leaving the band. I took a year off to do my own spiritual growing and searching, not knowing if I would ever be "good enough" to minister for God again, but also knowing that I could no longer deny my sexuality. Well, God opened a door, and it's been an amazing roller coaster ride ever since, and it has been *awesome!*

The fact of the matter is that the Bible has been used for centuries to oppress people. The Bible was used to support slavery. It's a known fact that the Southern Baptist church split from the original Baptist church because they believed the Bible supported slavery. Women have been oppressed, and scripture has been the basis. The Bible was used to support the notion that the earth was flat, and when Galileo came along and said the earth was round, the church wanted to kill him for blasphemy! Well, we all know the earth is round, and the church was wrong. The church has had to apologize many times for its misinterpretation of scripture, and I am seeing many other denominations doing the same today. The gay community is yet another community that has been oppressed and cut off from the body of Christ.

When we decipher the difference between an "act of sin" and a "state of being," I think we make the first major distinction when it comes to this issue. Lying, cheating, stealing, adultery, etc, are all *acts*. Homosexuality is a *state of being*. For example, a heterosexual isn't only heterosexual when they are having sex. They simply *are* heterosexual. For so long, a homosexual act has been what constituted being a homosexual. This is simply not true. Your orientation is what it is, whether you are sexually active or not. Acting upon your orientation on the other hand is a choice for anyone, gay or straight.

This is where I have issues with people saying they have "changed" their orientation. I believe those who have "come out" (maybe use different term, since "come out" is so associated with announcing one's homosexuality?) of the homosexual lifestyle are still homosexuals. They simply have chosen a path where they don't act on their orientation. In my opinion this is living a lie and I don't encourage anyone to do so, mainly because I've seen so much destruction and turmoil and, ultimately, suicides, as a result. However, for some, if they simply cannot reconcile being gay, and the only way they feel they can be at peace or feel that they are in God's will is to get married, have a family, be celibate, etc, then I support that. This doesn't mean that their orientation has altered. They simply are homosexuals living straight or celibate lives. I believe some people may be capable of being emotionally and sexually fulfilled with either sex (bisexuality). If someone is bisexual, they can't say they have "come out" of homosexuality. They simply have the ability to be compatible with either sex. If someone is bisexual, it is a much easier road if they choose to be with the opposite sex and not have to deal with the issues they would if they were in a homosexual relationship. Because of this, I think most bisexual people tend to be in heterosexual relationships. I know I would. However, for me, my homosexuality is no different than my race. I know this hasn't been 100% scientifically proven, but I believe there will come a day where we will discover this.

I believe the gay community is here to usher in a new movement of reminding people of God's unconditional love—and we know, because we have had to go through hell to find it, because of what *others* have told us, and what *others* have believed.

Only you can decide for yourself what you believe. That's the gift of life. We don't have to agree. We can agree to disagree, but do so in love and compassion. I am blessed with a beautiful partner, both in life and in my music, deMarco. As we travel and share our story and song, we make this very clear. We have to stop the hate. We have to stop the judgment and condemnation. We have to stop the killing. When will we "do unto others as we would have them do unto us"? When will we love our neighbors as ourselves, with no "ifs"? It doesn't say "love thy neighbor as thyself if they are straight, if they are white, if they are a man, if they are pretty, if they are talented." It says *love*, period. And *pray*. Pray that God reveals Himself to all of us on our journey, but first and foremost, pray that God reveals Himself to *you*, on your journey, that you may know His truth, and always come back to *love* in the end. Our world will be a much better place.

People are killing themselves every 40 seconds because they feel their lives are worthless. Teenage suicide is the third leading cause of death among 15–24-year-olds, and out of those kids, those questioning their sexuality are five times more likely to attempt suicide than their heterosexual peers. The church doesn't want to deal with this. They don't even want to acknowledge that it exists. They don't offer programs. If a kid goes to his youth pastor, he or she is looked at as possessed, disgusting, "not good enough" to be used by God. It's easy for the church to say what they believe, but are they willing to help people *deal* with the issue in a healthy way, not telling them they need to change or be "delivered," but loving them enough to allow them to search and find their truth in a healthy, safe space of love, compassion, and understanding?

Well, deMarco and I hope to provide that space for thousands, and we believe it's our call to do so. Door after door keeps opening for us, and God is in the center of it all. Just listen to our CD "songs for the spirit" and then ask me how we know God has blessed us, and our relationship, and how we know this isn't a sin. The Spirit of God is so present in that CD that people have literally said that at times they see a mist when listening to it. This is how the world will know. It won't be through long emails trying to justify or educate people or debates or long lectures, it will be through simply *living* our life, singing our songs, and allowing God to do what God does best. It is through the fruit of our Spirits, of our life, that people will know us—through joy, peace, compassion, harmony. Most of all, they will know us by our *love*.

I always thank people for their questions. We are all on a search. I'm sure there is a reason why God has placed this issue on your heart. Nothing happens by mistake. Maybe you are about to face a situation where someone you know and love is dealing with this issue, and trust me, when it hits you close to home, you will have an entire new way of looking at things. It's easy to tell another how you think they "should" live and what they "should" believe, but when you have walked in their shoes, you see things from a much different perspective. Perhaps you are going through this issue yourself and are beginning your journey of reconciliation.

I encourage you to just choose to love in every instance, as Christ came to show us, and let God deal with the hearts of others. And more than anything, pray that *Thy will be done.*

Jason Warner and his partner deMarco DeCiccio are life partners and make up pop duo Jason & deMarco. While their music has broad appeal, it has especially touched thousands of gay, lesbian and transgender Christians. This essay was adapted from a longer essay that Jason has posted on the bands website www.spiritpop.com. Jason and deMarco both welcome emails from fans. You can reach them through their website.

Healing from the Broken Truth

by Darlene Kay Bogle

As the leader of an Exodus International Ministry for several years, I received and listened to hundreds of phone calls from men and women who struggled with their sexual orientation. Many of those people came from Evangelical and fundamentalist churches, and had been told in person or from the pulpit that they were an abomination to God, and unacceptable to the Church because of their desire for same-sex relationships.

I received the calls because I was a minister of a broken truth. I had been part of the gay community for many years, but with my connections to ex-gay ministry, extensive prayer healing sessions, and a strong will to not be rejected by the God who loved me and gave Himself for me on the cross, I thought I was free from homosexual desire. That was the truth I spoke out on national television and wrote about in articles and several books. I proclaimed that truth, and shared that pathway to every caller, offering hope for them to share in the promised land of freedom.

There was only one problem. Many of the calls were repeat calls from gays and lesbians who followed the prescription to sexual freedom and were still stuck in the land of broken truth. They wanted to be free from same-sex attraction, and had read their Bibles faithfully, but they still had the desires. The dreaded question always came into the conversation.

"How long did it take you to be free from attractions to women?" My mouth responded, "I make the choice every day to avoid situations of temptation."

My heart cried out, I long for the comforting arms of a woman every day.

"Do you ever want to be in a relationship with a woman"? The questions were honest and personal.

I lied.

I thought they needed hope for change, and I was a minister and a director of an ex-gay ministry. I was a national speaker. I was also involved with a woman and had dedicated my life to her on every level.

I lied.

Oh, I was creative in my lie. "My relationship with the Lord is the most important thing in my life."

That was true. "I know that we are all responsible to Him for our behavior in life."

That, also, was true. "I know it's hard not to act on sexual desire when it feels so right. God can give you the strength, even if the desire never changes."

Well, that was true too; it just wasn't true for me. *I can't share with you that God has brought a Christian woman into my life and it is His gift to us to be a couple.*

I shared a broken truth with those who called or visited the ministry, because that is what we were all teaching at Exodus ministries and in support groups across the country. Our truth had been passed on by well-intended theologians for years, and Bible teachers who needed homosexuality to be a choice so that it could be a sin. We had the cure for sin, actually; Jesus died for our sin and we knew how to preach that truth. However, these were Christians who were calling me. They wanted truth that would set them free.

And again I lied.

One of the definitions of truth is "a judgment, proposition or idea that is true or accepted as true." I had been convinced for years that proclaiming change was possible, and that living that out in my life would make a difference for others. The only problem was that God had brought this Christian woman into my life and I was more whole than I had been with all the prayer, healing and deliverance sessions over the past dozen years! I was scared to tell the whole truth to my callers, or to my peers in ministry.

All the years of not wanting God to reject me for being gay and wanting to be accepted by my peers in ministry kept me paralyzed from telling the whole truth.

I longed to share with my group, and all those who called me looking for "help," that being gay was not a choice, that it was God's gift and they were welcome to come into the presence of God and celebrate who He had created them to be. I longed to encourage them to awaken their spirituality and their sexuality as a part of their sacred creation by a loving, compassionate God.

My partner Des and I discussed my conflict and she asked one simple question: "If you are convinced of this truth, then why don't you share it with others? God will not reject you, and there is no one else in the entire universe that matters." She paused. "These are your brothers and sisters in Christ and they cannot repent of who God created them to be. You have a responsibility to encourage them with the eternal truth of God." She reached over and took my hand. "Darlene, you and I are blessed in our faith and we have a godly relationship. The fruit of the Spirit is evident in our lives and that is the confirmation of God's approval upon our lives and our love."

From that time forward, I began to share God's loving acceptance as I had experienced it. I spoke truth to the people God brought into my life. I encouraged men and women to take a stand against the prejudice that would diminish them as God's children, but to do it in love. The debate about being Christian and gay will rage as long as there are theologians who feel they know God's mind on such topics. However, we who know and embrace the Heart of God will grow in our understanding of the truth that sets us free, not a fractured truth that casts us away from union with the Almighty. God loves us unconditionally and created just as we are, to be the man or woman He has called us to be.

My exit from Exodus is taking me on a journey of walking in forgiveness toward those who believe differently. Even those in our own families sometimes choose the broken truth of what they have been taught from the pulpit, rather than choosing to love their child unconditionally. It is no wonder that so many of the GLBT people want nothing to do with Christianity or a God that is represented by their judgmental families and churches. I know that I am a unique, royal priesthood, a Holy Nation; the only me that there is in the entire world, and that God is proud to call me daughter. My journey allows me to embrace my brothers and sisters in the gay community and invite them to celebrate their sexuality and their spirituality as they too embrace the God who says, "Come unto me all you who labor and are heavy laden, and I will give you rest."

Exodus International still offers broken truth to broken people. Their journey of healing into the Promised Land of heterosexuality is strewn with the causalities of despair and hopelessness, shame and rejection; and for those not strong enough to battle the prejudice, a growing number of suicide victims. There are those who mask their pain of rejection with promiscuity or chemical dependency, looking for love in all the wrong places. Their hope for the Promised Land of heterosexuality is an illusion.

My voice is small against the world of evangelical rhetoric and prejudice condemning the gay and lesbian community that dares embrace a vital faith with the Living God. My voice is small, but as truth begins to ring the bell of freedom and celebration, I am joined by thousands of other voices, gay and straight, and from every faith persuasion across the land. Men and women who see a whole truth of unconditional love and embrace it for themselves and for their loved ones are speaking out.

My prayer is that love will continue to enlarge the borders of our hearts and lives until we stand in unity, without shame or blame, and rest in the truth that the battle is not ours, it is the Lord's. My faith in Jesus is unshaken. He has already made the way for each of us to be filled with His love, and celebrate with abandon as we embrace our love and share it with the world.

Darlene Kay Bogle (left) is the author of A Christian Lesbian Journey: A Continuation of A Long Road to Love. *She lives in San Jose, California with her partner and welcomes your emails at darlenebogle@darrenmain.com.*

Two Thousand Years Later

by Darren Main

Jesus came down off Mount Sacajawea of the Bridger range and entered the city of Bozeman in the state of Montana. As he entered the town, people from the whole of Galitin County came to hear him preach.

Jesus said, "Blessed are you who are oppressed on account of the color of your skin, for your physical appearance is an expression of the Divine.

"Blessed are you who have been told that your path home is wrong and still endured, for your faith has brought rest to a tired world.

"Blessed are you who have found the joy of a loving relationship regardless of your orientation, for your love brings peace to the world.

"Blessed are you who have been driven off the land which God has given you to protect, for your love of the earth shall endure.

"Blessed are you the mothers, daughters, and sisters who have been treated with disrespect, for it is your joy to give birth to the Divine, and bring hope to the future.

"Blessed are you who have not been oppressed, yet felt the pain of seeing your brothers and sisters crucified on my account, for you know what it is to be a child of God.

"But Woe to you who have used the guise of religion to oppress people of color, for you have missed the chance to see the face of God.

"Woe to you who have misused my teachings to lead people from the path of their heart, for in doing so you have become lost.

"Woe to you who have condemned the love of any two people, for you have guaranteed emptiness in your relationships with others as well as with God.

"Woe to you who destroy the earth for worldly treasures, for you have not seen the heavenly treasures which present themselves in the simple beauty that surrounds you.

"Woe to you who have only known women as objects, decorations, and entertainment, for you have denied your own heart the opportunity to be tender, nurturing and loving.

"Woe to you who have called your brothers weak on account of their gentleness, for you have exchanged the power of God for the weakness of mortality.

"O City of Bozeman, remain faithful to what you know to be true. God is within you. Therefore, love the lord your God, and love your neighbor as well as yourself. In this right thinking you will create a community free of hate!"

Note: I wrote this while I was living in Bozeman, Montana. There had been a rash of hate crimes by "Christians" around that time. This story was my response to that hate.

Resources

Appendix A
Recommended Reading

Living in Sin: A Bishop Rethinks Human Sexuality by John Shelby Spong

What the Bible Really Says About Homosexuality by Daniel A. Helminiak

God is not a Homophobe: An unbiased look at Homosexuality in the Bible by Philo Thelos

Jesus, the Bible, and Homosexuality: Explode the Myths, Heal the Church by Jack Rogers

Stranger at the Gate: To Be Gay and Christian in America by Mel White

Religion Gone Bad: The Hidden Dangers of the Christian Right by Mel White

The Children Are Free: Reexamining the Biblical Evidence on Same-sex Relationships by Jeff Miner and John Tyler Connoley

New Testament and Homosexuality by Robin Scroggs

Sexual Conversion Therapy: Ethical, Clinical and Research Perspectives edited by Ariel Shidlo, PhD, Michael Schroeder, PsyD, Jack Drescher, MD

Anything But Straight: Unmasking the Scandals and Lies Behind the Ex-Gay Myth by Wayne R. Besen

A Christian Lesbian Journey by Darlene Bogle

Coming Out Spiritually: The Next Step by Christian de la Huerta

Appendix B
Recommended Films & Music

God and Gays

www.godandgaysthemovie.com

Luanne Beck's groundbreaking film on queer Christians.

For the Bible Tells Me So

www.forthebibletellsmeso.org

A powerful documentary exploring the effects of religious bigotry on four families.

Priest

A movie exploring the struggles of a Catholic priest who is torn between his calling to serve the Church and his being gay.

Latter Days

A sweet romantic comedy about a Mormon boy who falls in love with another man.

Jason & deMarco

www.jasonanddemarco.com

A musical duo and gay couple that have seen firsthand what religious intolerance is like and lived to sing about it! They are a great inspiration to GLBT people everywhere, especially young people.

Appendix C
Queer-friendly Organizations and Websites

Affirmation   www.affirmation.org
An organization supporting queer Mormons

U.M. Affirmation   www.umaffirm.org
An organization supporting queer members of the United Methodist Church

Born Different   www.borndifferent.org
A website with easy-to-understand science about homosexuality (not to mention a cute dog named Norman who moos instead of barks). Great for adults and teens.

Cathedral of Hope   www.cathedralofhope.com
One of the world's largest queer Christian churches

Dignity USA   www.dignityusa.org
An organization supporting queer Roman Catholics

Evangelicals Concerned Inc. www.ecinc.org
An organization supporting queer Evangelical Christians

Gay Church   www.gaychurch.org
An online directory of queer-friendly churches as well as other resources for queer Christians.

GLAD   www.glad.org
Legal support for the queer community.

Human Right Campaign   www.hrc.org
The largest queer civil rights organization in the USA.

Inclusive Orthodoxy   www.truthsetsfree.net

A website devoted to dispelling myths about homosexuality while maintaining orthodox Christian views of theology.

Integrity   www.integrityusa.org

An organization supporting queer Episcopalians.

LYRIC   www.lyric.org

An organization supporting queer and questioning youth. Staffed largely by other queer young people, this is a great resource for young people who need support.

PFLAG   www.pflag.org

An organization supporting the friends and family of queer people. Many resources for family members struggling to accept their loved ones sexual orientation.

Q-Spirit   www.qspirit.org

A community of spiritually minded queer individuals from many spiritual traditions from the East and from the West.

Rainbow Baptists   www.rainbowbaptists.org

An organization supporting queer Baptists

Rainbow Christians   www.rainbowchristians.com

An online dating and social networking resource for queer Christians.

Religious Tolerance   www.religioustolerance.org

An expansive website with many articles and resources about homosexuality.

Soul Force   www.soulforce.org

An organization that seeks to "cut off homophobia at its source—religious bigotry" by following the "principles taught by Gandhi and Martin Luther King, Jr. to peacefully resist injustice and demand full equality for LGBT citizens and same-gender families."

Steps to Recovery from Bible Abuse
www.otkenyer.hu/truluck/index.html
A website and book designed to help individuals and groups heal from the abusive programming directed toward queer individuals.

American Psychological Association www.apa.org
Information on the most current research available regarding queer psychological and emotional issues.

Teach Ministries   www.teach-ministries.org
Out of the pain of losing her lesbian daughter to suicide, Mary Lou Wallner started this ministry to assist other Christian family members in supporting their queer loved ones.

The Gay Christian Network   www.gaychristian.net
A nonprofit organization providing resources and support to queer Christians. The GCN also works with churches and religious groups.

United Church of Christ Coalition for LGBT Concerns
www.ucccoalition.org
An organization supporting queer members of the United Church of Christ.

Welcoming Churches   www.welcomingchurches.com
An online directory of churches that welcome gay, lesbian and transgender people.

Whosoever Magazine   www.whosoever.org
An online magazine for queer Christians.

DARRENMAIN.COM

- Find Darren's schedule of classes and events
- Download and listen to Darren's talks (no charge)
- Read Darren's articles on yoga, health and modern spirituality
- Search a directory of yoga studios
- Subscribe to Darren's podcast, "Inquire Within"
- Sign up for Darren's quote of the day and eNewsletter

Inquire Within Podcast

Inquire Within is Darren's podcast (Internet radio program) in which he interviews leading voices in the fields of holistic health, progressive politics and modern spirituality. It is free and you can download it at www.darrenmain.com or sync it automatically with your iPod through the iTunes music store.

Lectures and Book Signing Events

Darren travels throughout the United States and abroad. Please visit www.darrenmain.com for a current schedule of events. If you would like to host an event at your yoga studio, church, bookstore or community center, please send an email to events@darrenmain.com.

Nonprofit Fundraisers

Darren frequently offers fundraising events such as workshops, book signings and lectures for charitable causes. Please visit his website for more details and to find out when he will be in your area. You can also request information on fundraisers by emailing events@darrenmain.com

Acknowledgements

Special thanks to my family:
My mother Kathy Ascare
My father John Main
My brother Jason Main and my sister Jennifer Main
My nieces Zoe Main, Haley Joe Holdridge and Lauren Glaza and my nephews, Chase, Jake and Tyler Flynn
Don, Amy, Alden, Josie, Joe, John, Sarah, Peter, Linda, Kate, Gus, Adelina, Arthur and Mary, and all the other Mains who are too numerous to mention.

Special thanks to the many friends who have supported me so much:
Lance King, Michael Lynch, Christopher Love, Jasper Trout, Michael Watson, Sue Louiseau, Stan DeBoe, Wanda Pierce, Brian Lyttle

To my editors:
Kim Hedges—Thank you so much for your tireless efforts in editing my words in this book and in everything I write. You have the patience of a saint to be able to deal with my spelling!
I would also like to thank my editing team: Angie Ryan, Michael McComber, Jason Baxter, Kathy Martin, Caley Joyner, David Kresner and Russ Gregg.

Special thanks to Jasper Trout for creating such a beautiful cover for this book.

I would also like to thank Thierry Bogliolo and all the staff at Findhorn Press. Without their faith in my writing, none of my books would have been possible.

FINDHORN PRESS

*Books, Card Sets,
CDs & DVDs
that inspire and uplift*

For a complete catalogue,
please contact:

Findhorn Press Ltd
305a The Park, Findhorn
Forres IV36 3TE
Scotland, UK

Telephone +44-(0)1309-690582
Fax +44-(0)1309-690036
eMail info@findhornpress.com

or consult our catalogue online
(with secure order facility) on
www.findhornpress.com